MAKING MARKETS

Recent Titles in
Contributions in Economics and Economic History

MAKING MARKETS
An Interdisciplinary Perspective on Economic Exchange

Robin Cantor, Stuart Henry,
and Steve Rayner

Foreword by
AMITAI ETZIONI

PREPARED UNDER THE AUSPICES OF THE OAK RIDGE
NATIONAL LABORATORY

CONTRIBUTIONS IN ECONOMICS AND ECONOMIC HISTORY,
NUMBER 135

Greenwood Press
WESTPORT, CONNECTICUT • LONDON

Library of Congress Cataloging-in-Publication Data

Cantor, Robin Ann.
  Making markets : an interdisciplinary perspective on economic
exchange / Robin Cantor, Stuart Henry, and Steve Rayner ; foreword
by Amitai Etzioni.
    p.   cm.—(Contributions in economics and economic history,
ISSN 0084–9235 ; no. 135)
  "Prepared under the auspices of the Oak Ridge National
Laboratory."
  ISBN 0–313–26821–5 (alk. paper)
  1. Capitalism.   2. Markets.   I. Henry, Stuart.   II. Rayner,
Steve.   III. Oak Ridge National Laboratory.   IV. Title.
V. Series.
HB501.C2422   1992
338.6—dc20   91–42731

British Library Cataloguing in Publication Data is available.

Library of Congress Catalog Card Number: 91–42731
ISBN: 0–313–26821–5
ISSN: 0084–9235

First published in 1992

Greenwood Press, 88 Post Road West, Westport, CT 06881
An imprint of Greenwood Publishing Group, Inc.

Printed in the United States of America

The paper used in this book complies with the
Permanent Paper Standard issued by the National
Information Standards Organization (Z39.48–1984).

10 9 8 7 6 5 4 3 2 1

To Joan and Dan

Contents

Foreword: The Socioeconomics
of Markets

Free competition (the market) is the core macro concept of the neoclassical view of the economic world. It is typically viewed as free standing and self perpetuating. Behind various formal definitions and mathematical notations is a well-known idea: Adam Smith's notion that as each actor in the market pursues his or her own goal, the result will not be destructive conflict but, on the contrary, an automatically harmonious and self-perpetuating system. Moreover, the exchanges—which are what the market is all about—will organize the use of resources in a maximally efficient manner without outside intervention.

In contrast, socioeconomics sees competition, the market, and indeed the economy, as a subsystem nestled within a more-encompassing societal context. In addition, it assumes that competition is not self-sustaining; its very existence, as well as the scope of transactions organized by it, is dependent to a significant extent upon the contextual factors—the societal capsule—within which competition takes place. *Making Markets* focuses on the institutional structures that sustain various different patterns of economic exchange. This perspective locates the work in the socioeconomic tradition that views both the societal capsule and competition as differentiating concepts and as variables in the sense that, unlike perfect competition (which either exists or is absent), encapsulated competition exists in varying degrees and forms, some of which are more constructive than others.

The socioeconomic concept of competition is a social-science, cybernetic, system theory. Here, too, behind formal terms and theorems, lies a core idea: competition is a form of conflict, namely contained conflict. In contrast with Adam Smith's assumption of an invisible hand, socioeconomics assumes that the divergent interests and pursuits of various individuals do not automatically mesh together to form a harmonious whole. Hence, specific mechanisms are needed to protect competition, to keep conflicts within limits, and to prevent conflict from escalating to the point of self-destruction. The societal context that limits the scope of competition is not merely a source of market constraints, but is also a precondition for its ability to function. In this book, an economist, a sociologist, and an anthropologist look at the social context containing economic activities through the rules that govern demand, supply, and the conduct of legitimate transactions.

The subsystems at issue are neither fully competitive nor uncompetitive, but vary in the scope of behavior organized by competitive rules. For example, competitive rules govern more relations among strangers than among kin and are considered in many societies to be more appropriate for commerce and sports than for social relations. Within the contemporary American economy, competition is stronger in some sectors (e.g., within the restaurant industry) than in others (e.g., among electrical utilities). Societies also differ in the effectiveness of the mechanisms that contain and sustain competitive behavior.

To develop a workable concept of market exchanges, the authors move beyond the conceptual opposition between "free competition" and "government intervention," which implies that all interventions are injurious and that unshackled competition can be sustainable—dichotomies that are the curse of intellectual and scholarly discourse. Typical is the notion that competition is voluntary and hence good. This disregards the fact that most exchanges occur among nonequals in economic, social, and political power and hence are partially coerced. By the same token, government is often considered coercive and therefore bad, something that overlooks the fact that government is often persuasive or uses economic incentives rather than force and that the capsule is only partially governmental. Competition, like rationality, ought to be treated as a differentiating concept; the question is what levels of competition (especially as measured by the scope of the activities it encompasses) are efficient and in line with one's values, rather than destructive.

According to the socioeconomic line of argumentation advanced here, competition, as a mode of conflict, can be preserved only within some collectively set limits or context. This is true for all modes of conflict;

for instance, national values that agitate against civil wars set the boundaries for tolerable intrapolitical strife. Economic competition is no exception. For example, values prohibit the use of violence or illicit activities (such as industrial spying) among competitors.

At the same time, one must also establish the conditions under which the very same factors that sustain competition, by keeping it within bounds, themselves infuse the realm defined by society as the legitimate zone for competition, violate its autonomy, and undermine the ability of actors within the zone to follow its logic. In short, like a nuclear reaction, properly bounded competition may be viewed as a major constructive force; when unleashed it is highly destructive; and when repressed it is likely to lose its power or even be extinguished.[1]

Rules are needed to preserve not merely the competition but also the competitors. Fully unfettered competition leads corporations to cut short their investment in research and development (R&D), capital assets, and maintenance, and puts pressure on them to employ illicit or illegal means (or both). This could lead to either the destruction of numerous competitors and "innocent" third parties, or a catch-as-catch-can "war" that forces the community to reintervene. Such a war would result in a concentration of economic power and the end of free competition. Those who are committed to competition in the longer run must therefore support its being a partially limited, rule-governed conflict.

Does all this constitute a call for rule setting? It calls for recognition that the world is complex and allows more than just two alternatives: simplistic endorsement of unfettered competition or a blanket support for rules. Socioeconomic analysis ought to focus on the following questions: How many rules are beneficial, and which facets of which economic activities can be ruleless without undermining the values to which the common people are committed, including that of maintaining competition? Among the dichotomies that hinder serious intellectual examination, few are as detrimental as the notion that free markets are good and governments are bad, because some measure of rule setting and enforcement is clearly needed but too much is harmful. In their conclusion on sustainable development, the authors of *Making Markets* agree that the main way to form and sustain rules is to build up the moral values and commitments of a community rather than expand government or unleash competition.

By formally delineating the range of options, this contributes to the debate over the appropriate mix of competitive, coercive, and cooperative rules governing market exchanges in relation to both institutional development and the availability of physical resources. In the following chapters we see that the free competition/government intervention dichotomy is too simple. Real economic exchange takes place along a

spectrum of increasingly constrained conditions. The authors have il-
luminated this spectrum by detailing eleven different sets of exchange
conditions.

Therefore, Cantor, Henry, and Rayner join others in the socioeconomic tradition who argue that the proper question is not, Which ideal
type as exchange system wins your endorsement? but rather, What is
the most productive mix, given various value (goal) assumptions?

Amitai Etzioni

NOTE

1. The line of analysis advanced here draws on previous sociological analyses
that treat the economy as a whole (and not merely the competition) as a subsystem "bounded" by, or "embedded" in, the social system (Etzioni, 1965;
Granovetter, 1985; Parsons and Smelser, 1956; Polyani, 1944; and Swedberg,
1987).

MAKING MARKETS

1

Introduction

The question underlying this book is, "What is a market?" That the question seems banal may be why we were unable to find a satisfactory definition of the market in the social science literature. The definitions available to us from the disciplines of economics, anthropology, and sociology were either so general as to include all exchange or so specific that they excluded activities typically thought characteristic of markets. If the market, based on the interplay of individual buyers' and sellers' self-interested decisions, is the best way to distribute goods and services, and the collapse of centrally planned systems in Eastern Europe and the Soviet Union seems to confirm this, then it is not unreasonable to expect social scientists to provide an adequate general definition of the market process. Oddly, in all of the invective among anthropologists, economists, and sociologists on the topic of economic exchange, no one has criticized the others for this failing. Before we attempt to redress the lack of an adequate definition of the market and to flesh out its various manifestations, it is worth dwelling for a moment on the view of markets traditionally taken by each of the three disciplines and the criticisms that economics, anthropology, and sociology have leveled at one another.

THE VIEW FROM ECONOMICS

Economists conventionally define the market as the activity in which buyers and sellers exchange goods, services, and money and where prices and quantities are determined through the forces of supply and demand. There may be any number of buyers or sellers and a variety of products. Markets may range from the formal and organized to the informal and loose-knit. They may be episodic, intermittent, casual, seasonal, or continuous. While not necessarily limited to a particular place, markets range in extent from domestic to local and from regional to national and international exchange. Economists often classify markets according to the type of good or service transacted, as in the industrial market for manufactured goods, capital markets for long-term funds, or, in a specific sense, as in the sugar market. Another variation is based on the segmentation of demand, as in the youth market, while another is based on the location of traders, as in export markets or regional markets.

We will examine the economists' attempts to define markets and economic exchange in more detail in chapter 2. Here we seek only to explore some general issues that arise when economists confront other disciplines with this view. For instance, anthropologists and sociologists often criticize economists for reducing complex human social processes to an abstract form. Indeed, perhaps most repugnant to many of these critics is the economists' tendency to see all values in monetary terms and, therefore, subject to market exchange principles. Critics have argued that monetization of values does not work for understanding some exchanges (Henry and Mars, 1978; Gaughan and Ferman, 1987). Perhaps more importantly, conventional economic reductionism ignores the centrality of social institutions like the family in creating the psychological conditions favorable to the emergence of the inner-directed, self-reliant individualism of a market economy (Lasch, 1977). Economists such as Julie Nelson argue that the traditional emphases of economics correspond to a masculine approach and ideology (Nelson, 1992). Feminist economics places more emphasis on the responsibility and dependence of economic agents. By ignoring the social basis of exchange and its structuring by political interests at a group and class level, economists often fail to capture the complexity that is social life and with it such realities as "sharing without reckoning" (Roberts et al., 1985).

From the anthropological perspective, the most general criticism of the application of economics to noncapitalist societies is the ethnocentric assumption of individual reward maximization as the universal motivation for exchange. Moreover, sociologists and anthropologists have reasons to be skeptical that this assumption is consistently appropriate to advanced capitalist societies (Faberman and Weinstein, 1970; Davis,

1972; Cheal, 1988; Etzioni, 1988). The economic paradigm for decision making is highly individualistic and may not reflect the collective process that is prominent in many societies. Related to this objection is the accusation that economists tend to abstract market behavior from other political and social relations in which it is clearly embedded (Brenner, 1987). From the standpoint of economics, such relations, when recognized at all, tend to be viewed as irrational obstacles to the proper functioning of a free and efficient market.

Anthropologists also object to ethnocentric assumptions in the construction of data by economists (Hill, 1987). For example, comparisons of "household" statistics may be systematically misleading because of an economist's tendency to define a household according to his or her own experience of the nuclear family. In Africa, in contrast, polygamy not only breaks the family into multiple households, but various members of such a family may have very little idea of the extent of assets controlled and economic activities engaged in by other relatives. Even in Western industrial societies the economic activity of the household is composed of many more strategies and varieties of provisioning than traditional economics allows (Burns, 1977; Illich, 1981; Gershuny, 1983; Pahl, 1984)

Related to this criticism of the conception of microeconomic units, critics take economists to task for their willingness to believe that bad quantitative data are better than good qualitative data and, further, that explanation is more valuable than understanding. Yet the statistical information available on most developing countries is not merely confounded by respondent ignorance or concealment of their household resources but also by systematically distorted data collection methods. Many statistical profiles of developing countries reflect only the official economy, when the informal sector may even exceed the former in scale and local importance, such as in Lima, Peru, Bombay, India, and Djakarta, Indonesia, where it provides over half of all jobs, or in Belo Horizonte, Brazil, where it provides two thirds. Worse still, many statistics are little more than the guesses of less than impartial government officials.

Another shortcoming of economic modeling raised by the critics is the tendency to direct theory and models to address only the representative individual, household, or firm. The emphasis on the representative case is misleading where differences in the market participants define the economic problem, such as corporate culture and worker productivity or family structure and investments in education or technical skills.

Finally, most economists are criticized by sociologists, anthropologists, and even a minority of their own profession for assuming the scarcity of resources. Economists are concerned with the allocation of resources whose scarcity is given rather than determining from the allocation of resources whether or not they are, in fact, scarce (Redclift, 1987).

THE VIEW FROM ANTHROPOLOGY

Not surprisingly, anthropologists, too, suffer from their own disciplinary myopia, the limits of which economists are often quick to point out. Chief among these is the propensity to emphasize the uniqueness of the particular societies in which they work and to resist generalization. Recently, this tendency has been raised to a general principle within U.S. anthropology that limits cultural analysis to a commentary on the performance of an indigenous culture but ignores social organization or linkages with wider society and rejects comparison among cultures. Ulf Hannerz describes this trend aptly: "Agent, individual, self, action, experience, performance, all have the sound, in these 1980s, of the vocabulary of a yuppie anthropology" (1986:365).

This emphasis on the particular uniqueness of societies tends to make anthropologists resistant to the systematic modeling of economic behavior; to a similar degree economists tend to overlook significant differences among societies in pursuit of universal models. In contrast to economists, anthropologists view the market as one of a variety of exchange processes and not necessarily the most significant one. Rather than seeing the market as a universal dimension of human behavior, they see it as one form of exchange embedded in a particular culture that shapes motivations for producing, exchanging, and consuming goods and services. Different cultures value different goods and services and regulate different kinds of relationships among those who produce, exchange, and consume. Thus, anthropologists focus on the social relationships created by the exchange of goods and services (Mauss, 1925; Davis, 1972) rather than on prices and profit.

Importantly, anthropologists also distinguish the market from the marketplace, which is the physical location in which market exchange occurs. Because most people do not make their living by selling goods or their labor on the market in many nonindustrial societies, the market, as understood by economists, is the mechanism used for allocating only a limited range of resources. Even when it does operate, traders seek to reduce their risks by developing special relationships with each other, and this in turn tends to change the nature of the exchange from market type to one based on expectation and obligation rather than on price (Mintz, 1961; Davis, 1973).

In contrast to economists, then, anthropologists' emphasis on the differences among societies, the priority they give to exchange, and the difficulties in making cross-cultural comparisons leads them to refute attempts to monetize values and to downplay the market in their analysis. When anthropologists do pay attention to market behavior, they tend to understate the economic importance of markets by comparison with institutional and symbolic aspects. In general, anthropologists may be guilty of ignoring what economists take as the central reality in order to celebrate the marginal, peripheral, and even the frivolous.

THE VIEW FROM SOCIOLOGY

Like anthropologists, sociologists also prefer the more general concept of exchange to the specific form of the market. Sociologists share anthropologists' concern with the meaning attributed to market relations within specific situations of social interaction. However, anthropology sees the cultural context as preeminent, whereas sociology considers the historical organization of society at both a macro- and a microlevel to be the critical defining factor.

Sociologists conventionally view market exchange as part of the evolution of society from precapitalist to modern industrial society. This evolution has been characterized in a variety of ways: from status to contract (Maine, 1861), from gemeinschaft to gesellschaft (Tonnies, 1887), and from mechanical solidarity to organic solidarity (Durkheim, 1893). Although differing in specifics, all of these grand evolutionary schemes propose a qualitative difference between historical (and contemporary primitive) societies and the modern world. The world of the ancients is characterized by a simple division of labor; relationships based on kin-based status roles, such as mother and child or siblings; and communication dominated by informal, personal relations. In contrast, the modern world is characterized by a complex division of labor, the alienation of labor from individuals through the development of relationships based on contracts, and formal decision making based on technical and economic goals of rationality and efficiency.

Karl Marx and Max Weber differed in their judgments of the role of the market in this evolutionary process. Marx saw this development as one in which the formally free market for labor concealed a property owning minority that had the power to employ those without property. For Marx, market exchange and price mechanisms were means by which elites exercised power rather than means for individuals to pursue freely their own self interests. On the other hand, Weber saw the market as liberating people from the limited roles allowed by their status in families or clans to become sellers or buyers of goods, including labor. However, as sociologists evaluate the transformation from ancient to modern society, most persist in the conviction that the two are fundamentally distinct with respect to economic exchange and the exercise of power. Indeed, sociology as a discipline has differentiated itself from anthropology and history largely by renouncing the study of premodern societies. In modern societies, sociologists largely concede the arena of economic exchange to economists while concentrating their own attention on the exercise of power through social class (and, more recently, race and gender).

Indeed, this tendency is a fundamental failing of much mainstream sociology. Sociologists are so concerned with abstracting patterns of behavior, and categorizing these as groups, classes, or other social categories forming a hierarchy of power, that they neglect the human agents whose decisions and action, rational or otherwise, constitute the very structures sociologists describe. In U.S. sociology this tendency has been reinforced by the dominance of quantitative approaches and statistical techniques that are susceptible to many of the same criticisms as those economists who believe that bad quantitative data are better than good qualitative data and explanation is more valuable than understanding. The result is that the sociologists' constructs, such as class, are then taken to have causal significance, while the human agents are rendered passive actors and cultural dopes. Little wonder that some critics have argued that "the mistake is to assume that men are as sociologists have typically described them" (Filmer et al., 1972: 155).

Some sociologists imbued with a respect for ethnographic inquiry and a celebration of the socially constructed nature of meaning would seem to avoid this trap. Like their anthropological counterparts, however, they tend to analyze industrial societies as a plurality of conflicting subcultures with little sense of the wider sociopolitical context that economists and mainstream sociologists might claim really drives human behavior and social action.

CLASHING VIEWS ON DEVELOPMENT AND THE ROLE OF THE INFORMAL ECONOMY

Of course, this brief summary of economic, anthropological, and sociological perspectives on economic exchange does not do justice to those who have attempted to overcome the limitations of a single discipline by reaching into those of their neighbors (Becker, 1976; Douglas and Isherwood, 1978; Leibenstein, 1976; Williamson, 1975, 1985). Such writers are in the minority, however, and even they tend to borrow only those concepts that are nonthreatening to the central paradigms of their own disciplines. For the most part, economists tend to focus on price, income, and profits as the chief explanatory variables; anthropologists tend to focus on interactive social networks; and sociologists tend to focus on larger scale forces of political demography as the source of explanation.

There can be little wonder, therefore, that anthropologists, economists, and sociologists concerned with development issues have held one another in long-standing mutual disregard. Anthropologists, who are accustomed to long-term immersion in a culture, may dismiss as superficial the prescriptions of development economists who fly into the capital of a developing country for a few weeks to advise governments on their policy for tax reform or trade. Economists may tend to regard anthropologists as the romantic recorders of dying tribal cultures that present obstacles to policies of rational development. Sociologists often regard both disciplines as stooges to the political machinations of class, gender, and ethnic power.

Furthermore, each discipline is guilty either of largely ignoring the significance of informal economies, particularly among urban populations, or of reducing them to fit their own disciplinary paradigms. Those economists who have considered the phenomenon seriously have tended to view the informal sector as a profit maximizing response to burdensome government control (Gutmann, 1977; Bawly, 1982; but for an enlightened economic view see Roberts et al., 1985). Anthropologists, for their part, have been guilty of excluding economic motives in favor of the ritualistic role of the informal economy in the development of social and political networks (but see Hart, 1973). Sociologists, too, have been seduced by the very power structures that they seek to criticize by conceiving of informality as marginal or even as a political creation rooted in a social structure that has been shaped and sustained by the state (Weiss, 1987; but see Henry, 1988 for a less dependent view).

Another failure of anthropologists in approaching development issues is that they tend to concentrate on these solely in the Third World context (but see Portes et al., 1989). Yet, the issue of sustainable development, which we shall explore in this book, requires that we understand the relationships between micro- and macro-socioeconomic processes as part of a world system in which all countries are seen as developing, and potentially competing for, access to renewable and nonrenewable resources.

For a short while following World War II, there was considerable interest among anthropologists in the incorporation of traditional societies into the modern world economy as independent nations. Important and interesting questions were raised about the compatibility of traditional kinship structures and economic competitiveness in international markets. Alas, however, economic anthropology was sidetracked into an internal reproduction of the sterile opposition between anthropology and economics described earlier. *Formalists* in economic anthropology essentially argued the case of economists for simple universal models of rational exchange, while *substantivists* continued to insist on the incommensurability of economic activity in different cultures. Likewise, for many years economic sociology was overshadowed by its roots in psychological behaviorism (Homans, 1961). This was considerably redeemed by a more economically oriented structural exchange theory (Blau, 1964). More recently, a new direction has emerged in economic sociology typified in the work of Etzioni (1988).

One response to the debate in anthropology and sociology was the exploration of Marxist economic perspectives, which could have provided an alternative paradigm. Alas, the Marxist alternative found its own backwater in these disciplines. In economics and sociology, Marxism spawned theories of economic dependency that laid all responsibility for underdevelopment at the doors of greedy developed nations. For example, the long-standing Marxist view that colonial social systems were precapitalist or feudal was, in recent years, replaced with the view that peripheral colonies were integral to the development of Western capitalism (Frank, 1967) and that these formed part of a world or global system (Wallerstein, 1974, 1979). This view is a tempting perspective for South America and Africa, but one that totally ignores the counter examples of the Pacific dragons: Japan, Korea, Hong Kong, Taiwan, and so forth. Indeed, it was criticized for its economic assumptions, which defined capitalist social relations in terms of market relations rather than in terms of capitalist modes of production and the social relations that these entailed (Brenner, 1978). In anthropology, Marxist theory soon degenerated into obscure debates about the correct number of modes of production to be found in the Marxist liturgy.

The losers from all of this disciplinary bickering have been the global economy and, more recently, the global environment. These losses have been especially acute in those developing countries where falling per capita incomes have been accompanied by increasing environmental degradation since the 1970s. Modern economic and environmental problems will require interdisciplinary approaches to find solutions.

PROSPECTS FOR RECONCILING APPROACHES: THE IMPORTANCE OF PRICE SIGNALS

Economists, as well as anthropologists, have criticized development economists for their indiscriminate emphasis on macro solutions to what they see as microlevel problems. In contrast, sociologists have criticized development economists for their reliance on a neoliberal market oriented capitalism that "seeks to change attitudes toward self-employment and enterprise while restructuring national and international markets more in favor of large corporate enterprises" (Gerry, 1987: 119). Where anthropologists have pointed to institutional and cultural variation and sociologists have highlighted the inevitable reproduction of structures of power, however, the internal critique from economics is that development studies have paid insufficient attention to microeconomic issues, especially price signals from markets (*The Economist*, 1989). In our view, the concept of signaling may provide the piers for a potential bridge between anthropology, sociology, and economics.

Anthropological recognition of the existence of diverse market structures and sociological identification of power structures can be reconciled with a microeconomic perspective provided that all three disciplines are prepared to recognize that prices are not the sole signaling mechanisms that are of importance in markets and that demand for goods and services is not the only relevant message in the market place. Sociological concerns over the concentration of power and its ideological masking can be reconciled with microeconomic and anthropological views, provided that there is recognition that microlevel units do not exist in a vacuum. They are shaped by macrolevel forces and individual choices are only free after considerable channeling through sociopolitical structures.

Exclusive emphasis on the concept of price as a signal of scarcity recognizes only one form of communication in exchange behavior: the transmission of information. We can borrow from the field of risk communication to illustrate the implications of such a limited concept of communication. Most risk communication studies are concerned with the formulation, transmittal, and reception of a quantitative message about the probability and consequences of an unwanted event. The analogy of message transmitter and receiver in risk communication is between buyer and seller in the market. Risk managers, however, are often disappointed when they cannot conclude a sale (obtain risk acceptance) even when the price (risk) is lower than that of other comparable goods. The reason is that, while the quantitative signal is important, risk communication is also an issue of constructing a shared meaning about the world among those who generate and those who bear the risk. Important components of this shared meaning include processes for establishing trust, distributing liabilities, and obtaining consent to the whole package of societal concerns accompanying the numerical risk estimate. Similarly, social status, a dimension of market activity typically regarded as external to economic exchange in whatever forms this takes (e.g., class, gender, ethnicity, age), may be involved in the process of establishing a convergence of meaning between buyer and seller. Put simply, signals about relative social status may be just as important to market mechanisms as monetary prices.

This book is the product of collaboration among an economist trained in neoclassical theory, an anthropologist who has specialized in cultural interpretation, and a sociologist who has conducted considerable research on informal economies. From the outset, our intention has been to develop a genuinely interdisciplinary approach to the phenomenon of exchange of goods and services among human populations under diverse socioeconomic conditions and resource environments. To our way of thinking, interdisciplinary research inevitably is problem driven.

It is the process of bringing diverse disciplines to bear on the definition of a problem at its inception that distinguishes interdisciplinary research from merely gathering multidisciplinary perspectives on a problem defined by a single discipline. The problem that brought us together initially was the question with which we began this chapter, "What is a market?" We soon began to elaborate this initial question, however, by asking: "And what is the role of the market in sustainable human development?"

THE CHALLENGE TO MARKETS IN SUSTAINABLE DEVELOPMENT

The challenge to development economics is more powerful and important than ever. Our concern can no longer be limited to the development of the Third World. The debt crisis and economic migration to developed countries are just two manifestations of economic global interdependence. The issues of stratospheric ozone depletion and global climate change from the burning of fossil fuels and deforestation are clear signals of our environmental interdependence. Economy and environment themselves are inextricably linked as causes and effects. Local environmental degradation often is a consequence of poverty and excessive population concentrations. Yet the efforts of countries to develop their way out of poverty presently indicate increasing fossil fuel use leading to global environmental degradation. At the time of this writing, China and India are refusing to eschew chlorofluorocarbon refrigerants that deplete stratospheric ozone without economic assistance from the developed world. This is another sobering example of the linkage between economic development and environmental protection.

Sustainable development is the often-touted term for the proposed solution to these interrelated economic and environmental issues. As the mind boggling extent of environmental degradation in Eastern Europe and China becomes clear, it is evident (contrary to Communist ideology) that command economies, which subsidize resource extraction and encourage waste, are environmentally less desirable than market systems. These observations reinforce the current preference in the United States and many other developed countries for market-based solutions to environmental problems through the internalization of so-called environmental externalities.

Environmental externalities arise when the cost of damage to the environment caused by an activity is not reflected in the price of the goods or services produced. For example, the emission of particles from the smokestacks of large manufacturing facilities or the pollution from private cars are forms of waste disposal that are free to the operators, who might not even be aware of the environmental costs of their actions that must be borne by society as a whole. We recognize, therefore, the need to develop markets where they do not exist and the need to correct environmental market failures where markets do exist. Yet, we are operating without any adequate definition of the market and with a narrow and impoverished conception of the role of markets in the development of social and institutional life!

Market systems also have proven themselves to be superior at providing societal wants. The inefficiency of centrally planned economies was a major motivation of the reformers of the 1968 Prague Spring. It was a standing joke in Czechoslovakia that because the production targets for screw factories were set by weight alone, it was impossible to get a small screw in the whole country. Following the collapse of communism throughout Eastern Europe, Poland, eastern Germany, Czechoslovakia, Hungary, Romania, and the former Soviet Union are all seeking to develop market economies. The developing countries also are tending to move away from centrally planned or highly interventionist economic systems, partly because of the obviously superior economic performance of countries with market systems and partly because of pressure from development banks and aid donors.

The problem that Eastern Europe and the developing nations face, however, is how to build effective markets where the necessary institutional framework has not had the opportunity to evolve historically or where such institutions have been eradicated by central planners or even natural disasters. The problem is particularly acute in cultures where relevant information contained in existing exchange behavior cannot be reduced simply to price signaling. This may be because exchange relationships not only signal prices but also are important for communicating prestige or building social solidarity in or among communities. These dimensions of exchange are of particular importance to the traditional indigenous systems of exchange in many developing countries, as well as among informal economy networks in more industrially developed centrally planned systems.

A further dimension to the problem of the contribution of markets to sustainable global development is the need for such a strategy to be applicable at extreme levels of social scale. Local implementation of environmentally and economically sustainable strategies is essential to deal with problems that result from the cumulative impacts of individual and family activities. The level of face-to-face interactions, however, must be capable of being articulated to the actions of regional and national governments and, ultimately, to international forces. In other words, "How can the concept of markets help us to articulate the connections between local and global thought and action?"

INTERMEDIATE MODELS: A COMPARATIVE MICROECONOMICS?

One plausible response of social theorists to these challenges could be to develop a variety of models of different sorts of markets. In other words, at the intermediate level of abstraction between the extremes of anthropological empiricism and macroeconomic universalism we could create a diverse comparative microeconomics. This would be a microeconomics that includes a variety of signaling functions, additional to price, and one that can be understood to serve multiple functions—holistic social and political development criteria—rather than just money-based wealth production. Comparative capability could be preserved by paying attention to the common need for rules constituting various aspects of exchange activity, even while the actual rules produced by different markets in response to the need for rules might be quite diverse.

To establish any sustainable economic framework, a range of functions must be performed, either by the market itself or by the institutions that regulate or engage in economic exchange. The social-science literature has identified at least fourteen such functions, eight of which are primary or constitutive functions in that they collectively comprise the exchange activity. A further six functions are secondary or emergent functions in that they are not essential to exchange at its inception, but as exchange persists they will emerge, usually as instruments of increased efficiency. All fourteen functions are listed below:

Primary functions:

1. Define property rights
2. Convey supply/demand information (including advertising)
3. Provide opportunity for legitimate transactions
4. Limit provisions of legitimate contracts
5. Enforce contracts other than by physical coercion
6. Settle disputes
7. Maintain civil order
8. Legitimate other functions

Secondary Functions:

9. Guarantee currency and close substitutes
10. Administer distributive justice, including taxation

11. Monitor and modify operations in response to changing circumstances

12. Mitigate risk

13. Exploit comparative advantage, specialization, and division of labor

14. Reduce transaction costs for intertemporal or interregional transactions (e.g., through credit)

In subsequent chapters we show how the choice of rules for fulfilling each of these functions gives rise to a continuum of ideal typical exchange structures. These range from highly constrained nonmarket systems based on the social obligations of membership in a network, such as an extended family, through perfect competition in which all exchanges are freely and anonymously negotiated in the market, as in the model of neoclassical economics, to market systems that themselves become constrained, not by traditional obligation but by unequal market power. In each case, the rules for fulfilling the exchange functions define the exchange structures.

In this book, our approach to the application of these ideal typical models (packages of rules) to various conditions of development or redevelopment is, at this stage, a formal exercise that incorporates information about natural resource constraints as well as institutional constraints on development. At this point our efforts begin to infringe on the relationship between economics and the environment, although we are aware that we presently fall far short of the sort of socioecological model that could result from the path we have begun to tread. We are also acutely aware that we are limited to essentially static models. A next step in this research program (though not necessarily for the present authors alone) could be to develop rules of transformation from one exchange structure to another.

INSTITUTIONS AND RESOURCES

The original study on which this book is based was concerned with the prospects for establishing market economies following a major societal disaster on the scale of nuclear war or a major regional disaster such as an asteroid collision or an earthquake (Cantor et al., 1989). This assessment, however, stimulated us to examine the most basic issues of human exchange of goods and services at all levels, from the intimacy of the primitive family to the anonymous markets of contemporary capitalism.

Thinking about societal recovery from severe damage to its resources and its institutions of economic exchange led us to address issues of resource availability and institutional capability that are relevant for any discussion of economic and social development irrespective of origins in societal disaster, such as nuclear war; global underdevelopment, such as besets much of the African continent; or economic stagnation, such as in the previously centrally planned economies of Eastern Europe. As well as addressing the viability of exchange arrangements under extreme combinations of institutional infrastructure and resource endowments, this book is also about a new approach to economic thinking because, in seriously confronting such radical circumstances from an interdisciplinary perspective, we were forced to rethink and revise some of our cherished conventional economic and social assumptions.

Throughout this book, we attempt to be explicit about the general theoretical assumptions that constitute our approach, as well as the limitations that we have placed on the scope of our inquiry. We seriously question monolithic approaches to applied economic analysis and policy based on what works under existing conditions. By being forced to consider how exchange and markets may emerge in radical circumstances, we were obliged to challenge many taken-for-granted assumptions. In short, we have had to reexamine how people make markets where governmental institutions, existing resources, and market confidence are absent or severely restricted.

We believe that an interdisciplinary approach is necessary to transcend the myopia of existing assumptions about institutional arrangements and narrow disciplinary thinking. We also believe that a rules-based approach to examining the process of exchange will facilitate the analysis of economic evolution because it separates an exchange institution into its components and, thereby, allows us to think about how particular rules may be changed within the institution rather than assuming the complete replacement or reconstruction of institutions. By separating out the necessary functions for economic life, we are able to see how alternative institutions may perform similar critical functions in different systems.

The development literature is dominated by studies that advocate the transfer of Western market orientated practices, while largely ignoring the development issues of building the institutional infrastructure that supports these practices. Essentially, these studies take for granted the important institutional functions of industrialized countries that comprise the market process. We prefer to begin by elaborating different starting conditions for the development process, each of which presents a particular set of problems to be overcome. We examine the way an economic environment is affected by various levels of development in regulatory systems, banks, stock exchanges, enforcement agencies, and resources such as land, products and machinery, labor, skills, and knowledge. We identify critical combinations of these components of institutional infrastructure and resource endowments to identify four deductive scenarios that are defined by the relative scarcity or availability of resources on the one hand, and by the degree of development of exchange institutions on the other.

FOUR DEVELOPMENT SCENARIOS

We specify a range of scenarios for economic activity and the development of various combinations of ideal-typical exchange structures. These scenarios are based on the assumption that resource endowments (skills, goods, and information) and institutional infrastructure (the social mechanisms that organize production, regulate exchange, and maintain trust in contracts and currencies) vary greatly in different socioeconomic contexts. While various directions of economic evolution are possible, to facilitate analysis we hypothesize the following four ideal typical logical possibilities: (1) "Business as Usual" as in the industrialized West, in which both institutions and resources are highly developed as in the contemporary U.S. economy; (2) "Wasteland," in which both resources and institutions are highly restricted, as in some areas of the Third World; (3) "Fat of the Land," where the resources are plentiful but the institutions are severely restricted, which also may be the case in developing countries; and (4) "Bureaucratic Nightmare," where resources are very restricted but the institutional infrastructure, including government, remains extensive, as, for example, in the Soviet Union and the transitional economies of Eastern Europe.

Our analysis makes the highly artificial assumption of a closed system and considers economic development as it could be driven largely by domestic resources and institutions. We identify economic development not solely in terms of a modern industrial market economy but as the achievement of a sustainable system of production and exchange that lays the conditions for subsequent economic and technological development. However, this sustainable system is what we consider to be the minimum requirement for economic arrangements that stimulate market processes. We do not define economic development as the achievement of modern industrial capitalism but as achievement of a sustainable system of production and exchange that satisfies the conditions necessary for subsequent economic growth and technological development.

Our aim in later chapters is to discuss the kind of market and exchange activity each scenario would possess given our starting assumptions. We consider these scenarios in relation to empirical evidence about exchange activity in a variety of historical and geographical settings, to suggest how various rules of exchange are modified and institutions adapted or developed to perform necessary functions for economic life, such as maintaining trust or creating confidence in institutions to enforce contracts. In this way we seek to prepare the conceptual building blocks from which strategies to deal with real developmental dilemmas can be built.

2

Modeling Markets: A Common Framework for Analyzing Exchange

In this chapter, we will propose an interdisciplinary framework to study exchange activities. This framework is designed to be sufficiently general to facilitate comparison among different kinds of exchange, while remaining sensitive to incentives for exchange that extend beyond financial gain to include social bonding, status, and prestige. We will focus on sets of rules that describe demand, supply, and transaction options for any given set of exchanges. Differences in property rights, transaction costs, and the degree of choice over transaction options distinguish nonmarket exchanges, informal-market exchanges, and formal markets in this common framework.

IS THERE A GENERAL DESCRIPTION OF THE MARKET PROCESS?

The position that the market process occupies in the economics literature initially led us to assume that economists shared a clear consensual definition of the concept and its essential characteristics. However, as Brenner (1987) points out, this is not the case. At best, it can be said that most definitions of market processes fall into one of two categories: general exchange spheres and institutions free of collective action.

The category of general exchange spheres encompasses just about any form of voluntary exchange. For example, Alchian and Allen (1969: 63) define the market as: "a non-administered device allowing uncoerced parties to negotiate exchanges." Presumably, any exchange not administered by some central authority would be consistent with this definition. As another example, Schelling (1978: 23) describes a market as "the entire complex of institutions within which people buy and sell and hire and are hired and borrow and lend and trade and contract and shop around to find bargains."

The second category, institutions free of collective action, has been used by a number of authors to make a distinction between a market process and a contract process. Thus, these definitions focus on the differences between anonymous exchange and exchange relationships, defined either by contract or membership in an institution, like a firm. However, it would be incorrect to claim that the degree of this distinction is consistent in the literature. In fact, we can identify three views of the distinction between market and contract processes.

First is the view that markets involve decentralized decision makers attempting to coordinate their desires:

> Market institutions create a horizontal mechanism for coordinating economic activity between consumers and producers. Private property rights are generally decentralized, distributed among the individual actors, and market prices act as presumably low-cost transmitters of information, enabling potential trading partners to locate and contact one another. In addition, specialized traders, or middlemen, emerge to bring partners together, lowering transactions costs further. For many transactions, negotiating costs are negligible and enforcement costs are low, because self-interest is the enforcer. For other transactions, in which behavior is difficult to monitor or property rights difficult to define, negotiating of enforcement costs may be significant enough to inhibit trade. (Toumanoff, 1984: 535–36)

Thus, decision makers are decentralized, but middlemen (coordinators) are within the bounds of the market process. Consistent with this view are those analysts who see the perfectly competitive model as representative of the market process. For example, Hurwicz (1973) discussed "market phenomena" in connection with the Walrasian auctioneer process (i.e., a system of bidding where trade is allowed only at the prices that equate supply and demand in all markets) and a "command system" when referring to those supply and demand decisions made by a centralized authority. Arrow (1969: 69) refers to the perfectly competitive equilibrium as "a free market equilibrium." Such views would see competitive conditions as necessary for the market process where relative prices guide the exchange behavior of decentralized decision makers.

A second (and popular) view disregards collective action as long as it has no significant effect on the price system. This view is characterized by the attention given to the price system in the market process. One is left with the impression that for a market process to exist, all that is necessary is a price system with some flexibility to respond to demand and supply conditions. Bell (1981: 50) argues that this emphasis began in the writings of Alfred Marshall: "For Marshall, price theory was what economics was all about." Friedman (1976: 5) proposes that: "The fundamental principle of the market sector is the use of purchase and sale to organize the use of resources." Further, he noted: "The introduction of enterprises and money does not change the fundamental principle of a market system" (p. 6). In their book, *The Market System*, Haveman and Knopf (1966: 11) stated: "A market system is one in which the basic economic questions are decided, not by some central authority, but by producers and consumers acting in response to prices. The essence of the system is that the goods are produced for exchange and exchanges are money transactions." While this definition reflects the operation of many modern U.S. markets, it excludes transactions that are accomplished in the absence of either money or explicit price systems.

Finally, the third view is the most restrictive in the sense that it presumes a price system and requires that the identities of trading parties do not affect the terms of the trade (Williamson, 1979). Here, we have a distinction among three types of institutions for exchange: firms, markets, and relational contracting (Williamson, 1985). Firms are characterized by formal, hierarchical organization governing resource owners and employers. Markets are characterized by discrete, anonymous transactions. Relational contracting is characterized by flexible, time-dependent relationships between trading partners, as contained in implicit or explicit trading contracts.

One has only to contrast this last description with the definition of a general exchange sphere as almost any form of voluntary exchange to appreciate the lack of agreement on a single description of market processes. As another example to illustrate the diversity of definitions, Cheung (1983) argues that the market and the firm are merely different types of contracts.

The modern economics literature pays much attention to the components and outcomes of market activity but makes relatively little analysis of how markets emerge from social interaction (Gould, 1980). A related field is market behavior, which seeks to understand economic choice and how diverse activities and wants are coordinated by studying the incentives and responses of various social types referred to as market agents, such as consumers, producers, and laborers.

The literature on market behavior is closely connected to many of the original ideas set forth by Adam Smith in *The Wealth of Nations* (1776). In this seminal work, Smith identified the powerful force of self-interest and the equally powerful force of the competitive market process that lead selfish economic agents, as if guided by an invisible hand, to provide a diverse group of goods and services to satisfy the wants of consumers. Consequently, two paradigms of choice behavior that dominate economic modeling of exchange are utility maximization and profit maximization.

Smith's view of the market process has been modeled extensively and expanded in the modern economics literature, the most notable being the formal modeling of Smith's invisible hand theory and its welfare implications for the economy (Debreu, 1959; Arrow and Hahn, 1971). Modern economic theory states that under a specific set of assumptions, competitive market outcomes not only equate demand and supply plans but result in an outcome where no one person can be made better off without simultaneously making another person worse off (Pareto optimality). Further, once this state of "optimality" has been reached, there will be no internal pressures to move to another set of exchange plans, thus reflecting an equilibrium state.[1]

Unfortunately, the perfectly competitive model of exchange is based on very restrictive and somewhat unrealistic assumptions (Bell, 1981; Schotter, 1985). For example, it ignores the factors that Kirzner (1973) and Brenner (1987) identify as the prime movers for the market process; asymmetries in market information and uncertainty that give rise to entrepreneurial decisions and actively competitive behavior (rivalry). In the perfectly competitive model, competition does not imply actively competitive behavior. Rather, it denotes the absence of competition where economic agents act as passive price takers subject to the same information. In a later criticism Kirzner remarked:

> Economists have always emphasized the beneficial role of competition in market processes. Sad to say, neoclassical economics long ago developed a technical notion of *static* competition which is not only antithetical to that used in everyday layman's speech, but which, more seriously, fails entirely to appreciate the nature and enormous importance of dynamic competition. Not only did neoclassical economics introduce a meaning to the term "competition" which is almost the opposite of its ordinary meaning, but, in so doing, it diverted attention from market *processes*. (1981: 116, emphasis in original).

The competitive force in the neoclassical model is not that firms or consumers aggressively attempt to outperform other rivals, but that there are so many traders that no single trader has any measurable affect on the outcome of prices and quantities. This large-number-of-traders condition, while crucial to the perfectly competitive model, does not fit most actual market activities, where information is asymmetric, rivalry is evident, or both. Thus, in real markets, a large number of traders hardly seems necessary although, when coupled with symmetric information and other conditions, it may be sufficient for market behavior.

Markets displaying the characteristics of the perfectly competitive model may have sufficiently different characteristics to justify distinction from other exchange institutions. These characteristics, however, are not found in most of the activities that we would readily accept as market processes. Thus, distinguishing exchange activities on the basis of the characteristics of the perfectly competitive model seems gratuitous at best.

An alternative to searching for a general description of the market process in the literature explicitly concerned with operating markets is to look where formal market operation is precluded. The literatures on market failure and nonmarket allocations are relevant to the market process because they emphasize the conditions under which formal markets will fail to exist or are unable to achieve optimal social outcomes (Toumanoff, 1984). Three key concepts emerge from these literatures that bear on market processes and resource allocation: (1) transaction costs, (2) externalities, and (3) property rights.

First is the concept of transaction cost, or what Arrow (1969) calls the costs of running the economic system and Williamson (1985) calls the economic counterpart of friction. Transaction costs arise because announcing that you have something to sell may not be costless, finding a buyer may not be that easy, and even when you do, buyers' checks can bounce. Toumanoff (1984: 531) provides a concise summary of these costs: "Transactions costs occur as resources are used when trading partners attempt to identify and contact one another (identification costs), when contracts are negotiated (negotiation costs), and when the terms of the contracts are verified and enforced (enforcement costs)."

Second is the concept of externalities in consumption or production. Actually, as Arrow (1969) argues, market failure due to externalities is a special case of the general problem of transaction costs. Externalities exist where an individual's gain or loss from a transaction depends on the actions of others. Thus, pollution from a nearby city may affect the farmer's costs of growing crops and hence, the return on the farming activity. Efficiency could be restored if a costless bargain (one where the costs of making the bargain are insignificant) could be struck between the two parties, that is, bribe the city not to pollute as much or compensate the farmer for his or her losses (Coase, 1960).

In many cases, however, it is difficult to correct externality problems because decentralized decision making cannot achieve the appropriate coordination among participants. For example, Schelling (1978: 42) describes a set of transactions where, in the absence of appropriate information and through the processes of sorting, segregation, or integration, market processes fail to bring about the desired social results: "If everyone wants to stay at home and watch the crowds in Times Square on television, there will be no crowds in Times Square, while if everyone wants to join the crowd to be seen on television, there will be nobody watching." In such cases, some coordination of individual plans or better information on the plans of others can produce a better aggregate outcome.

A third concept from the literature on market failure (as well as from economic anthropology literature) is property rights. Property rights refer to the entitlements that define how resources may be used by traders. Because decisions regarding resources are interdependent, societies define and enforce rules to govern the use and consumption of scarce resources as an alternative to the possible violent competition of their members for these resources.

Two alternative systems for defining property rights are private property and common property. The major difference between the two systems is that under private property, rights are assigned primarily to the individual, while under common property, rights are assigned primarily to the collectivity. Contrary to what many economists and noneconomists may think, common property does not imply the absence of an entitlement system. The absence of entitlements would indicate an open-access system (Stevenson, 1984). Of course, hybrid systems are also possible (e.g., where ownership entitlements are defined but use entitlements are not).

While many conditions characterize the private property or common property cases, in their simplest forms they embody: (1) a principle for exclusion (i.e., who may use and manage the resource and who may not) (2) a principle for distribution of income, costs, or both arising from the use of the property; and (3) a principle for transferring the rights implied by (1) and (2) (Cheung, 1983). In addition, Umbeck (1981) reminds us that all property rights are based ultimately on the abilities of the owners (individuals or groups) to persuade others to respect these rights or at least to exclude those who will not.

Market Processes

The economics literature does not yield a clear description of market processes. The literature, however, does emphasize several important market characteristics. These are voluntary repeated participation by decentralized decision makers, a price system, large numbers of anonymous traders, self-interested motivations, low transaction costs, and private property rights. From these characteristics we are able to construct a definition of market processes, at the transaction level of exchange, to guide our remaining discussion. Five overall requirements are important to this definition:

1. Property rights define control over goods and services; although private property may be important, its absence does not preclude a market process, whereas absence of control over goods and services does

2. There is a desire to exchange

3. Transaction costs do not exceed the perceived gains from completing the exchange

4. Choice exists over trading partners, trading periods, or both

5. There is trust in the security of the transaction being completed in an atmosphere of noncoercion

A market process exists where these conditions are present for at least two or more traders.

The first requirement specifies that either private property, common property rights, or some hybrid, must be recognized, at least implicitly, between trading partners. Thus, theft is not legitimate in a market process because this implies the absence of a shared definition of the rights that establish control over goods and services. The second condition reflects what Alchian and Allen (1969) call the exchange proposition: Some difference in personal tastes, endowments, or both suggests the opportunity for traders to gain from an exchange. The third condition simply means that the exchange results in a net benefit to the parties after all costs are considered. The fourth requirement introduces the process of choice. Thus, pure command or traditional allocations involving no choice are not market processes. Finally, the fifth requirement rules out the use of violence as a mechanism to complete the transaction.

We find the above trading characteristics in widely varying degrees in real markets. Their presence indicates little about the existence or extent of competition, government intervention, or allocation outcomes. Thus, they can only be considered as providing part of what we require to model the exchange activities conducted within markets. So far, our discussion has not considered market organization (Plott, 1986).

Market Organization

Market organization refers to the exchange institutions that govern or constrain the market process. Unless these institutions are specified, any number of allocation outcomes are possible from the market process. Conceptually at least, these outcomes become well-defined within the descriptive models of particular markets. Thus, any description of a market process lacks realism without further specification of how it is constrained by social institutions. Brennan and Buchanan argue strongly that to understand the market, one must pay attention to the rules that govern its operation:

> With respect to the far more important economic interaction among persons, however, the rules governing individual behavior within such interaction are often ignored. Economists, themselves, have been notoriously negligent in this respect. Complex analytic exercises on the workings of markets are often carried out without so much as passing reference to the rules within which individual behavior in those markets takes place. Adam Smith was not party to such neglect; he emphasized the importance of the "laws and institutions" of economic order. (1985: 13)

Moreover, this attention to rules is valid even if we limit our interest to the workings of the popular notion of the free market perceived by many to be the best example of an unconstrained market structure. Schotter (1985) argues that the popular notion of the free-market prescription for organizing economic activities, while very different from the perfectly competitive model of economic theory, is highly constrained by rules. These include the imperatives: (1) preferences of the individual are the best guides to define value and welfare (consumer sovereignty); (2) people will act in their own best interest (utility maximization and profit maximization); and (3) an unbridled price system provides the best incentives for economic growth (laissez-faire).

The popular notion emphasizes rules promoting individual freedom to conduct commercial activities and, as a result, is more closely related to the idea of free enterprise. In contrast, the notion of the free market in the formal economic literature is related to the model of perfectly competitive exchange. The perfectly competitive model deals solely with rules enabling price competition. As Stiglitz remarks:

> It is now widely recognized that the nature of competition in market economies is far more complex (and more interesting) than the simple representation of price competition embodied in, say, the Arrow-Debreu model. Not only are there alternative *objects* of competition: firms compete not only about price but also about products and R&D. But, also, the *structure* of competition, the "rules" which relate the pay-offs to each of the participants to the actions they undertake, may differ markedly from that envisioned in the standard model. (1986: 339, emphasis in original)

Whatever notion of the free market is used, the analysis of an actual market requires understanding the structure of rules that govern demand, supply, and transaction options for a particular set of transactions. Borrowing from the experimental economics literature, we argue that all exchange can be modeled as a combination of rules constituting an exchange structure or what Smith (1986) calls a microeconomic institution. The set of traders is composed of participants, their resource endowments, and their knowledge endowments. The set of rights and obligations specifies the rights of agents to communicate in order to effect exchange, property rights, allocation rules, and cost-imputation rules. Thus, we may view an exchange structure as a set of rules that indicate the agents and the options that they are allowed in any transaction. By focusing on the rules at the transaction level, it follows that all market processes are governed by exchange structures. Further, many components of these structures, such as fiat money and business law, are created through largely collective or command authorities. Not all possible and observed exchange structures, however, produce the characteristic features that we link to market processes. In particular, many exchange structures are highly constrained in the choice over trading partners, transaction options (leading to high transactions costs), and property rights.

A COMMON FRAMEWORK OF EXCHANGE STRUCTURES

We derive the bounding variables for our framework of exchange structures from literatures on both market and nonmarket exchange systems. The literature on formal markets already has reached a high level of abstraction, while the literature on nonmarket exchange tends to be strongly empirical, borrowing whatever abstract or explanatory concepts it uses from economic anthropology. A multivariate model that specifies the rules governing demand, supply, and transaction options, however, can be derived from both literatures. Finding the appropriate balance of abstraction and realism is often posed in the planning problems of large, complex systems (Katzner, 1983).

Each exchange structure consists of a series of underlying rules constituting demand, supply, and transaction options. Before we can list the actual rules for each exchange structure, we must consider the concept of rules.

The rules that enable a market to exist are described as constitutive rules. These are rules, such as the rules governing the movement of chess pieces, that define certain human activities. Without these rules the activity, in this case a chess game, could not be said to exist. There may be other rules about how to do the activity well, for example, develop knights before bishops; but these are not essential to the game. These other rules, therefore, are not said to be constitutive but facilitative.

Constitutive rules may be prescriptive or descriptive. A prescriptive rule, such as "Thou shalt not kill," requires that the subject of the rule voluntarily behave in a certain fashion, to choose to commit or refrain from an act, as a condition of participating in the wider social activity. Refraining from murder (however it is defined locally) is a condition of

participating as a full member of any society. Of course, voluntary adherence to prescriptive rules is usually encouraged by the threat of sanctions, most dramatically by exclusion from the wider society, more often
by the imposition of deprivations. Chess players, for example, will not
accept challenges from those who cheat or persistently refuse to learn
the permissible moves. Serious offenders against social or criminal codes
may be excluded from the enjoyment of civil society or subjected to a
curtailment of liberty, depending on the nature and severity of their
offense.

A descriptive rule is not necessarily a constraint on voluntary behavior
but is an account of regularities in behavior irrespective of whether it is
voluntary, habitual, or entirely determined by forces that are beyond
the subject's control. Natural laws are invariably descriptive. Planetary
motion is not regular because Kepler's burdensome laws prevent planets
from behaving as they would otherwise. Natural laws, therefore, consist
of descriptive rules that are invariably empirical. That is, they are derived
by inference from observation.

The social and economic rules that constitute human societies may be
of two kinds. There are empirical rules that describe how people behave
(descriptive). These are derived by observation of the subjects but are
not necessarily known to or expressed by them. There are also normative
rules that represent the rule makers' conscious model of how a society's
members ought to conduct themselves (prescriptive). Study of empirical
rules often teaches us that the normative rules are more honored in the
breach than the observance, in which case we usually reconstruct empirical rules to describe the patterns of exceptions to the normative rules
that may be permitted (Edgerton, 1985).

In examining exchange and deriving the rules vectors that constitute
exchange behavior, we are interested primarily in empirical, descriptive
rules. In addition, the normative, prescriptive rules are of interest insofar
as they actually constrain or enable choice behavior and so coincide with
a descriptive rule of that behavior.

The complete series of rules for each market or exchange structure
consists of three types of rules: (1) demand rules, (2) supply rules, and
(3) transaction-options rules. Table 1 contains a generic example of the
complete series that illustrates the framework (Cantor et al., 1989). Note
that the rules depicted in the table are intended to suggest only what a
complete series may contain to characterize an exchange structure. Rules
may be added or subtracted from the list without diminishing the rules
perspective.

The demand rules regulate the types of traders that can legitimately
signal their intentions to obtain the good or service. Demand rules describe who may demand the good or service and how it will be consumed
(e.g., whether or not it will be shared within a consuming unit). Another

Table 1
Rules Vector for Exchange Structures

Rules Vector Notation:
$R_i(d_1,...,d_n,s_1,...,s_n,t_1,...,t_n)$

where $i = 1, ..., k$ (exchange structures within an economic scenario) ;
d_x = the demand rules, $x = 1, ..., n$;
s_x = the supply rules, $x = 1, ..., n$; and
t_x = the transaction rules, $x = 1, ..., n$.

DEMAND RULES:
d_1 Who may demand a good or service?
d_2 How is consumption to be shared?
d_3 Is the good or service divisible or indivisible? This refers to the durability of the good or to what extent its consumption represents a significant portion of the consumer's income.
d_4 Is demand for survival or status? This is closely related to when demand occurs and if it is an immediate need.

SUPPLY RULES:
s_1 Who may supply a good or service?
s_2 Where does supply occur?
s_3 When does supply occur?
s_4 Is supply storable?
s_5 Are there technical, institutional (other than vector rules), or natural constraints on supply?
s_6 What are the major uncertainties facing suppliers?
s_7 Is the product or service homogeneous or differentiated?

TRANSACTION RULES:
t_1 Who holds the title to property as it is recognized within the exchange structure?
t_2 Who holds the entitlement to use and manage the property? This is related to the condition of universality, where all resources are owned privately and all entitlements are completely specified.
t_3 Does the condition of exclusivity (where all costs and benefits of owning and using the property accrue to the owners) apply?
t_4 Does the condition of transferability (where all rights are transferable in a voluntary exchange) apply?
t_5 Does the condition of enforceability (where property rights are secure from involuntary seizure or encroachment by others) apply?
t_6 How are bids to buy made?
t_7 Where are bids to buy made?
t_8 When are bids to buy made?
t_9 How are offers to sell made?
t_{10} Where are offers to sell made?
t_{11} When are offers to sell made?
t_{12} What is the medium of exchange? How are goods or services priced?
t_{13} How are transactions legitimated?
t_{14} How are transactions enforced?
t_{15} How is information distributed in the exchange structure?
t_{16} How are adjustments made for externalities?

demand rule specifies whether or not the purchase represents a significant portion of the consumer's income (i.e., lumpiness in consumption), because this will indicate sampling or market-entry problems. Finally, we consider whether or not demand is for survival or status because this will affect the urgency of the demand.

The supply rules focus not only on who may supply the good or service but also on how the technology and inputs of production might imply particular supply conditions. Command rules may limit who may supply (e.g., formal licensing). Traditional rules may have the same effect (e.g., where only the son of a blacksmith may become a blacksmith). The inputs may affect the temporal or geographical conditions of supply. In other words, they may place limitations on when or where supply may be available. The production technology or physical characteristics of the good may affect its storage potential. Descriptive supply rules may imply limitations on how supply can be organized. For example, a natural constraint on the only source of a good or a crucial input to the good's production provides a condition favoring a monopolist in supply. Additionally, there may be technological reasons such that production is less costly at large levels of output (i.e., there may be economies of scale). Economies of scale are similar to lumpiness in consumption in that the presence of either condition implies a barrier to entry in the market by certain suppliers or consumers. In the presence of economies of scale, producers must be of a sufficient size to produce the good or service at minimum cost. In the presence of indivisibility in consumption, buyers must have a sufficient level of resources to purchase the good or service.

Two other supply conditions that may affect the rules governing the organization of supply are the major uncertainties facing suppliers and whether or not supply is homogeneous or differentiated. Supply uncertainties can act much in the same way as natural or technical constraints on supply. This is especially true where there is significant informational uncertainty making risk an important cost of supply. In the case of product differentiation, greater distinctions among products that fulfill similar demands may encourage greater rivalry as firms attempt to increase their individual market shares.

Many of the rules and conditions revealed in the demand and supply analysis underlie specific rules that govern transaction options. Transaction options are those choices over property rights, selling, purchasing, pricing, monitoring, enforcement, and information that are permissible in the recognized transactions for the good or service.

Rules that designate property rights include specification of who holds the title to the property, who holds the entitlement to use and manage the property, and who receives the costs and benefits associated with the use of the property. Exclusivity exists where all costs and benefits of owning and using the property accrue to the owner. Transferability exists where all property rights are transferable in a voluntary exchange. Finally, enforceability exists where property rights are secure from involuntary seizure or encroachment by others.

The selling and purchasing rules include specification of how, where, and when these activities may take place. For example, traditional business hours are, in effect, rules that determine when a consumer may make an offer to buy from the supplier. Rules regarding pricing can stipulate that prices are posted (i.e. fixed at least for the transaction), established through an auction or negotiation process decided prior to the consumption of a good, or decided after consumption. Additionally, rules may exist that limit the medium of exchange to be used to complete a transaction. This is particularly true for certain prestige goods that can only be traded for other prestige items.

Finally, transaction options may be limited by how transactions are legitimated and enforced. For example, regulation, laws, and customs may limit the legitimacy of exchanges that traders might otherwise desire to transact. Another limitation on the transaction options arises from how information is distributed in the exchange structure. For example, transaction costs will be generally higher for traders where buyers and sellers do not have access to the same information regarding the good or service. Finally, externalities may be present in the production or consumption of the good or service. These externalities may instigate additional rules to allocate the costs, benefits, or both of the externalities to particular economic agents. For example, regulation may be enforced to limit the amount of supply that can be produced by a seller who uses a polluting technology.

The model we propose goes beyond the traditional domain of economic market models, but as Friedman argues, such an approach is appropriate for the study of different types of economic organization:

> Economics, by our definition, is not concerned with all economic problems. It is a *social* science, and is therefore concerned primarily with those economic problems whose solutions involve the cooperation and interaction of different individuals. It is concerned with problems involving a single individual only insofar as the individual's behavior has implications for or effect upon other individuals. Furthermore, it is concerned not with the economic problem in the abstract, but with how a *particular* society solves its economic problems. Formally, the economic problem is the same for a Robinson Crusoe economy, a backward agricultural economy, a modern industrial society organized on a communistic basis, and a modern industrial society organized on a capitalistic basis. But these different societies use different institutional arrangements to solve their economic problems. Thus there is need for a different economics—or a different chapter in economics—for each kind of society. There turns out, in fact, to be much that is in common to the various chapters, but this cannot be

required in advance; it is rather, one of the conclusions of economic science. (1976: 2, emphasis in original).

Friedman's statement begs the question, How alike are exchange structures? Our framework is defined to be of sufficient generality to include exchanges in the financial, familial, or group membership spheres because the social phenomenon of exchange is common to all these activities. Yet, social science disciplines have more or less restricted each disciplinary focus to a single type. As a result, economists have not said much about exchange for social membership, power, status, or prestige, and anthropologists and sociologists have not said much about exchange for financial gain, with the notable exception of Simmel's (1907) exchange theory. But as Smith (1974: 320) notes, "Man's propensity to truck, barter, and exchange is but a special case of his propensity for social exchange in nonmarket and institutionally constrained market contexts." As a result, the leading sociological exchange theorists such as Homans (1961; 1964), Blau (1964; 1968), Emerson (1972), and Cook et al. (1983) have discussed exchange for power; and Blau in particular documented exchange for respect, social approval, and other nonmaterial rewards.

Some of the disciplinary boundaries separating the social sciences have begun to dissolve, largely because of the growing body of interdisciplinary and extradisciplinary research. Hirshleifer (1985: 53) observes that as this work grows, it increases the strength of the evidence that "There is only one social science." There remain, however, two conceptual areas where the disciplinary interpretations continue to clash and cause problems for a common framework: rationality and reciprocity.

Rationality

In conventional microeconomics, rationality in exchange involves two major components: the basic motivation for action and the decision-making process by which actions are selected. The first component, the motivation underlying exchange, refers to whether or not economic agents are motivated primarily by self-interest in their exchange behavior. Alternative motivations would be altruism and malevolence (i.e., the presence of intended maliciousness in actions). The underlying assumption for exchange motivation is not trivial because it bears directly on the perceived gains from trade. Economists have preferred the self-interest assumption on the grounds that the other explanations can be made consistent with it by redefining gain. Most often gains are still modeled as purely financial or material outcomes, however.

The second component of rationality in the economic literature refers to the process by which people select actions of exchange:

Rationality is an *instrumental* concept. In the light of one's goals (preferences), if the means chosen (actions) are appropriate the individual is
rational; if not, irrational. "Appropriate" here refers to *method* rather than
result. Rational behavior is action calculated on the basis of rules of logic
and other norms of validity. Owing to chance, good method may not
always lead to good result. (Hirshleifer 1985: 59, emphasis in original)

While this definition is uncontentious, the way in which it has been
applied in economic modeling suggests a much more narrow definition.
This narrower concept underlies descriptive models that assume that
economic agents seek to maximize utility or profits over the set of all
feasible actions. Decisions are labeled irrational when they fail to satisfy
certain rigid axioms of rational choice. But as Simon (1955) has argued,
this view of rationality ignores the burden it places on a person's ability
to reason and use information. Thus, it is more realistic to assume that
individuals intend to be rational but are limited in their abilities to do
so (Simon, 1961), especially given the social commitments of their associations with others (Blau, 1964).

To help understand the implications of different assumptions about
rationality, we find that it is useful to distinguish between outcome and
process rationality. Outcome rationality describes a calculated process
of choice by individuals in the pursuit of explicit ends. Decisions can be
described as if made by an individual decision maker (i.e., within an
individualistic, self-interested perspective). This perspective treats collective decision-making entities, such as households or firms, as if they
too were individual decision makers.

To select among alternatives within an outcome rational framework,
decisions are based almost entirely on the individuals' knowledge of
market information. Individuals make their decisions without recourse
to other individuals. In the event that decision makers encounter uncertainty, they tend to base their decisions on probabilistic estimates of
the possible outcomes. Whatever else individuals may be thinking, their
decisions will appear to be consistent with mathematical optimization
over the choice set. Finally, the factors influencing individual behavior
can be reduced to a set of single decision points, each of whose influences
can be considered as a separate entity. A similar concept exists in the
early sociology literature on exchange (Homans, 1961).

There are certain advantages to economics in the concept of outcome
rationality, despite its admittedly simple assumptions about social behavior. Because of the emphasis on the representative individual, it is
not necessary to describe fully the social system within which individuals
behave. This facilitates the development of models that designate the
degree, location, scheduling, and kind of interventions possible in various economic systems. It also allows for the construction of mathe-

matically elegant models whose predictive value can be determined easily.

The limitation of outcome rationality revolves around its inability to explain confounding phenomena embedded in the surrounding social and cultural context of decision making (Etzioni, 1988). Conventional microeconomic theory has relied on a sharp distinction among ends, alternatives, and decision techniques in choosing among alternatives, but choice is permitted only about alternatives rather than about ends or techniques. Yet, as Leibenstein (1976) points out, decision techniques may well be treated as legitimate variables without any loss of coherence to economic analysis but, rather, resulting in models that better reflect real world decision making. However, Blau (1964) also argues that humans in reality rarely pursue one specific outcome to the exclusion of all others, are frequently inconsistent in their preferences, almost never have complete information on alternatives, and are never free from the social commitments of associations that limit the available alternatives. For these reasons, the concept of process rationality offers a more comprehensive approach to analysis.

The assumption of process rationality is broader in scope than outcome rationality because the total social milieu of the individual is considered. Additionally, its focus includes the knowledge required by individuals in order for them to function in social systems that either promote or affect patterns of behavior. Studying the knowledge that these individuals have of social institutions, obligations, and expectations from negotiated interaction with others thus becomes the point of departure relative to the outcome rationality models.

To describe decision-making behavior under the assumption of process rationality we require a holistic framework. In this framework, elements tend to take on important attributes, or meaning, in relationship to all other elements being studied. Holism acknowledges that structured hierarchies of decision points must be hypothesized from a study of the relationship among elements. In other words, we must recognize explicitly that decisions are linked by more than just the passing of time.

The assumption of process rationality applies when economic agents may not have the freedom to choose over all the feasible actions where traditional rules apply. In fact, discrete exchanges may take place that are completely dictated by traditional rules of fixed allocations. This would be true where the individual has relinquished some freedom of choice for group membership. While the more aggregate action still involves choice (i.e., to belong or not) at the transaction level, choice over alternative options is no longer available.

Finally, many examples once perceived as irrational behavior in outcome rational frameworks are now being explained as responses to high transaction costs. In fact, transaction cost analysis provides the link that can reconcile the outcome and process rational views. For example, McClosky (1986) shows that historically English farmers scattered their holdings of farmland not because they were irrational, but because insufficient markets existed in the farmers' social environment for spreading risk. Transaction cost analysis has also been used to investigate the creation of firms (Coase, 1937), vertical integration (Williamson, 1975), issuing coupons that lower prices in repeat transactions (Crémer, 1984), as well as numerous other issues. Thus, we can resolve many of the problems raised by the outcome/process rationality debate by focusing on the rules defining the incentives facing economic agents rather than solely focusing on the behavioral motivations.

Reciprocity

Drawing on the anthropology of Malinowski and Lévi-Strauss, Gouldner (1960) identified two characteristics of what he described as the "norm of reciprocity" that governs all social exchange. First is the proposition that the more people exchange with one another, the more likely are reciprocal obligations to emerge and guide subsequent exchange. Second, the more such reciprocity is violated, the more the injured parties will seek to sanction the violators. Implicit in the use of this concept of reciprocity is the notion that reciprocal exchange need not be balanced or perceived as fair. Subsequent clarification of the concept was provided by Sahlins (1972).

Sahlins (1972) defines three levels of reciprocal exchange. Positive reciprocity exists where the trader provides a socially recognized higher value of goods than he receives. Negative reciprocity exists when the trader attempts to maximize his return regardless of any socially recognized limits, "the attempt to get something for nothing with impunity." Reciprocity is only balanced where the value of goods exchanged is recognized as roughly equivalent by both trading partners and other potential market participants. The traditional economic model of exchange has focused largely on balanced reciprocity where (at the margin) equivalent payment is an outcome of the transaction. In fact, Boulding (1978) distinguishes between reciprocity and exchange because the former implies a deep commitment or meaningful relationship among traders that extends beyond the transaction point. In actual transactions, however, we observe variation in the timing of payment (Henry and Mars, 1978; Faith and Tollison, 1981) and in the timing of price determination (Smith and Smith, 1985). The empirical evidence makes it difficult to deny the presence of other types of reciprocity in actual exchanges.

Certainly from a social-cost perspective, negative reciprocity underlies the notion of monopoly rents or violation of property rights. Positive reciprocity, although often regarded as a misinterpretation (Becker, 1976), remains a nagging attribute of many exchange activities. Rather than attempt to explain away the phenomenon of positive reciprocity, we find it fits very well into our exchange framework when we allow for the exchange rules associated with social bonding, prestige, and trust. Positive reciprocity creates a running debt balance (Mauss, 1925; Davis, 1972) between traders that provides an additional incentive for continued interactions and the display of good faith beyond that provided by the institution of balanced reciprocity itself. We can reconcile the nonmarket and market literatures by simple recognition of this principle. Hirshleifer (1985: 58) observes that the principle is quite universal: "Some willingness to forego selfish advantage, some element of genuine trust between trading partners or among business associates, almost always remains a necessity in the world of affairs."

Several authors (Sahlins, 1972; Lomnitz, 1971) have noted that the nature of reciprocity varies with the social distance between suppliers such that positive reciprocity occurs among family, kin, and close friends constituting a close-knit network (Bott, 1957) that can be measured according to a range of network-theoretic variables (Holland and Leinhardt, 1979; Gross and Rayner, 1985). The goods most frequently exchanged in such structures are labor services, especially rudimentary specific skills, and commodities produced by group members with common skills but at different times.

On the other hand, exchange in a monopolistic market structure is not characterized by close-knit networks but takes place between nonintimates, unconstrained by rules arising from social proximity. Whereas the purpose of exchange between intimates with similar endowments is the creation and maintenance of social bonds by a continuing balance of debt, the incentive for a monopolist to exchange is maximization of income and unregulated accumulation of personal wealth, power, and prestige.

A rules framework at the transaction level overcomes a major shortcoming of many economic models of nonmarket exchange by explicitly recognizing varieties of reciprocity, the transaction costs people face when making exchange decisions and restrictions on choice. We can allow for distinctions in the incentives to exchange and for distinctions in the allocation rules. In short, we do not simply redefine all goals as self-interested and all choice among alternatives as outcome rational as have many studies employing a higher level of analytical abstraction (Hirshleifer, 1985).

A TYPOLOGY OF EXCHANGE STRUCTURES

Our specification of the rules for nonmarket and market exchange is based on existing evidence from three fields of study. These fields include the literatures relating to the formal markets in economic theory, informal economic activity in sociology, and primitive markets and trading in undeveloped settings from anthropology where maintenance of civil order and the enforcement of contracts is, or was, uncertain or based on very different arrangements from those prevailing in the United States today.

Economic theory has focused on the activities that transpire in formal market structures. At the most basic level of inquiry, it is recognized that formal markets perform certain functions that facilitate their continuity or allow the operation of other markets. For example, formal markets serve to disseminate information to economic agents, signal opportunities to buyers and sellers, reduce transaction costs for intertemporal or interregional exchanges, and exploit comparative advantage, specialization, and the division of labor. Of particular interest in the study of formal markets is the analysis of market power, uncertainty, and externalities (i.e., those forces that would prevent a market from satisfying the conditions of pure competition).

At a more disaggregated level, formal market analysis examines questions regarding the conditions of exchange between economic agents. For example, frameworks that are concerned with decentralized exchange, media of exchange, and contracting between agents have obvious implications for an exchange framework. Among the useful insights emerging from the formal market frameworks are the concepts of auctioneers, middlemen, entrepreneurs, coalition formation, and bidding behavior. Further, these frameworks highlight the importance of coordinating wants in the presence of barter exchange, the efficacy of money (when goods are complex, involve large coalitions of traders, or both), and the gains expected from the introduction of money. Lastly, formal market analyses identify various problems involved in the negotiation, maintenance, and enforcement of contracts where asymmetric information and market power pose impediments to trade.

A number of neighborhoods populated by individuals excluded from formal markets have developed trading and exchange systems for goods and services employing a variety of skills (Whyte, 1955; Liebow, 1967; Dow, 1977). While some of these exchanges are criminal, many are not. They involve household production (Burns, 1977; Pahl and Wallace, 1985), employment of neighbors and friends, and the use of unlicensed craftsmen and unregistered business, forming an irregular or informal economy on the fringes of the formal market sector (Ferman and Berndt, 1981).

Informal economies develop a strong knowledge base that forms neighborhood learning webs and informal exchanges of skills (Ferman, 1968; Ward, 1981). Studies of low-income neighborhoods also show that such trading networks serve to integrate the community and provide a social fabric of mutual aid and support (Lowenthal, 1975; 1981). Other studies show that it is not only the poor that trade in informal exchange structures. Many employed professionals and craftsmen engage in informal work (Pahl, 1984). Finally, disillusionment with the established helping services and decline in the traditional systems of social support, such as the family, has led to an expansion of nonmarket exchange structures that promote self-help and mutual aid among group members (Katz and Bender, 1976; Robinson and Henry, 1977).

Evidence from the trading relationships exhibited by primitive economies can be superimposed on contemporary informal economy studies to suggest the rules likely to exist where both institutions and resources are dramatically different from the Western market economy. The primitive economy relationships often depend on the protection of traders by powerful patrons or blood brothers (Eisenstadt and Roniger, 1984). Studies of primitive rationing suggest that it does not depend on centralized authority (Douglas, 1958). Studies of the symbolic aspects of exchange, their relationship to the development of mechanisms of prestige and power, and the formation of political alliances (Pospisil, 1963; Strathern, 1971) may be important in any context where existing authority structures are destroyed or severely impaired.

Economic theory and studies of informal economies and primitive trading not only suggest alternative exchange rules that should be considered but also define three interdependent spheres of noncommand exchange structures: traditional, informal, and formal. Figure 1 shows these spheres and the specific exchange structures that are discussed by each field of study. (A more detailed delineation of the rules for each exchange structure can be found in following chapters and in Cantor et al. [1989].) We stress here that the notion of spheres is in no way intended to delineate these exchange structures as existing in isolation. The reality of social life is such that human agents are simultaneously members of different spheres of interaction and that particular transactions rarely occur exclusively in one or another "sphere." Rather, spheres are more accurately described as extremes of a continuum exhibiting a greater preponderance of particular exchange structures (Harding and Jenkins, 1989).

Traditional Exchange

The rules governing transactions, distributions, and allocations have very little degrees of freedom for individual traders in the traditional sphere. From nonindustrial societies, *subsistence exchange* gives us clear evidence that trust through social obligations enables exchange to occur in geographically restricted settings and in spite of low levels of technology, specialization, and resources. *Prestige exchange*, consisting of

Figure 1
Noncommand Exchange Structures in the Interrelated Spheres of Exchange

TRADITIONAL SPHERE	INFORMAL SPHERE
Subsistence	Intimate
Prestige	Associational
Peasant marketplace	Criminal

FORMAL SPHERE

Perfect competition

Imperfect competition

Oligopoly/oligopsony

Monopoly/monopsony

Bilateral monopoly

ritual transfer of certain restricted items held in high esteem, shows us (1) the importance of social bonds in facilitating exchange, (2) the role of reciprocity as a credit mechanism, and (3) how competition for status acts as an exchange motive. *Peasant exchange* shows how simple technology alone does not preclude production for trade in localized marketplaces.

Informal Exchange

The informal sphere is characterized by a combination of traditional and market allocation rules. The influence of network restriction, however, pervades these structures. *Intimate exchange* occurs in extended family networks, self-help organizations, cooperatives, and communes of industrial society. This type of exchange shows that under circumstances of need being able to demand goods and services requires that one be a member of a socially recognized kinship network. Here exchange occurs to reinforce social obligations and is not necessarily related to the timing of wants. Serving the needs of network members is a primary exchange motive. *Associational exchange*, a characteristic of industrial societies, occurs among friendship networks and work acquaintances and shows that motivations to obtain goods and services at below market prices, or those of short supply, can be intertwined with those of status and prestige. The *criminal* variant of the associational exchange structure is that in which the goods and services that are traded have been stolen, obtained by fraud, or are defined by the extra-market legal system as illegal goods. This exchange structure possesses certain restrictive rules specifically deriving from the need to avoid apprehension by society's regulators, such as the police, as well as from the organizational structure of criminal enterprises. In part, it is this illegality that constitutes the network, bringing together those who might otherwise have remained apart (Henry, 1978).

Formal Markets

Exchange structures in the formal market sphere are dominated by the actions of decentralized decision makers. Thus, network and traditional allocation rules give way to rules offering more options and choices to enable decision making by self-interested anonymous traders. Under *perfect competition*, the rules of entry enable large numbers of buyers and sellers to have equal access to the market, and thus, to act as price takers with essentially no market power. In this structure, transaction costs must be of no significance and consent and enforcement of contracts are guaranteed by the availability of many alternative trading partners. In contrast, *monopoly* and *oligopoly* are characterized by substantial market power being vested in a single or small number of traders. Rules restricting market entry, the mobility of resources, or both, often result from high transaction costs due to price searching, risk reduction, indivisible products, or asymmetries of information. (We also recognize the cases of product demanders who themselves have market power.) Far less significant market power is present in the *imperfectly competitive* exchange structure, where rivalry among many similar producers leads to strategic behavior to increase market share and product differentiation.

CONCLUSION

Although central to any analysis of economic recovery or development, the market process remains a poorly defined concept in the economics literature. Our definition seeks to combine some of the salient characteristics associated with market analyses to capture the decentralized, uncoerced nature of market activities. Following this, we have developed an analytical framework that is not restricted to transactions that are strictly market oriented; rather, it is derived from the more general conditions and rules of exchange activities. As a result, the framework extends beyond the notion that exchange is conducted solely for financial gain under the conditions of balanced reciprocity and considers incentives such as social bonding, social approval, status, and prestige. Both market and informal exchange structures can be examined and compared in this framework.

We can use the framework to consider exchange possibilities under different conditions of resource and institutional endowments. For example, we can consider the way an economic environment is affected by various levels of development in institutions (e.g., regulatory systems, banks, stock exchanges, and enforcement agencies), and resources, (e.g., land, products, machinery, labor, skills, and knowledge). We then can consider the economic conditions in relation to evidence on different exchange structures to suggest: (1) how various exchange rules might be modified and institutions adapted in the wake of major change in the institutional or resource levels or both; and (2) which exchange structures can sustain stable trading relationships and which structures cannot survive in the absence of deliberate collective or authoritarian intervention to either create supporting institutions or regulate exchange rules.

An analysis based on the framework can contribute to understanding the possibilities for economic recovery or economic redefinition in the wake of major social and political changes. These issues often are dominated by those who believe that there is a natural tendency toward the industrial market economy no matter what degree of change occurs in economic conditions. This position may not be helpful because it undermines a serious focus on: (1) the conditions people might actually face in the various scenarios that may follow a major shock to the social system; and (2) what effects radical changes in social systems, political structures, institutions, and resources have on economic life.

Similarly, the economic development literature is dominated by studies that advocate the transfer of Western, market-oriented trading practices while largely ignoring the development issues of institutional infrastructure that support these practices. The important institutional functions of Western countries that constitute market processes should not be taken for granted. This point is exemplified by the recent events in Eastern Europe and the Soviet Union, where radical shifts in institutional infrastructure have unmasked a significant mismatch between the established exchanges rules and those desired by the new political regimes:

It is much easier to ram people into the pen of totalitarianism than it is to coax them out again. To shove them in you announce that many of the decisions which individuals used to make for themselves will now be made by the instruments of the state; you set up those instruments; you send the disobedient to prison or the firing squad. To put the process in re-

verse—to persuade people to resume the responsibility for decision-taking
—is turning out to be far harder. . . . Incentives or not, 40 years of the
system . . . seem to have drained away something vital. Reforming governments pass laws to encourage the growth of the private sector, but
depressingly few new private businessmen step forward. The governments announce the break-up of the huge old loss-making state conglom-
erates, and tell the smaller new units to compete with each other; but most
managers go on doing exactly what they did before. Not many human
beings actually enjoy taking risks, trying unfamiliar things, working late
rather than going home early. Almost everybody of working age in Eastern
Europe has spent his life in a job which demands little except casual
obedience. When a system based on the issuing of orders suddenly barks
"Make up your own minds!" it is not surprising that the first reaction is
a stunned apathy. (*The Economist*, 1989: 5)

Our approach can be used to characterize exchange structures and
facilitate the kind of analyses needed for the problems identified above.
By disaggregating an exchange institution into its rule components we
may begin to compare across institutional types and think about how
particular rules may be changed within institutions. This is a more realistic approach to development and economic change than the complete
substitution of one institution for another. Before examining the evolutionary possibilities for exchange structures under changing and harsh
institutional and resource conditions, we discuss alternative exchange
structures in chapters 3 and 4.

NOTES

1. Two of the more important predicted outcomes of the competitive equilibrium are the self-regulating nature of competition and the efficient coordination
of supply and demand information.

The characteristic of self-regulation refers to two properties of the perfectly
competitive system. First, given some exogenous shock to the system (e.g., a
new, large oil field is found), the forces of demand and supply underlying the
competitive model will move the economy to a new price/quantity outcome that
reflects this new supply. The concept of self-regulation denotes the economy's
ability to adjust, without extra-market intervention, to a new equilibrium outcome (Arrow and Debreu, 1954). The same term also has been used in another
way when referring to the competitive model. The second meaning, which
emerges in the models of fully contestable markets (Baumol et al., 1982), principal-agent problems (Stiglitz, 1983), and the notion of consumer sovereignty
(Lerner, 1944), is related to the way competition regulates self-interested or
opportunistic participants to (1) do what they have promised and (2) produce
what people want at the lowest price.

Efficiency in the use of information and communication resources to bring
about the demand-equals-supply condition, rests entirely on what Hurwicz
(1973) calls the "mechanism for resource allocation." In the perfectly competitive

model, such a mechanism may take the form of an auctioneer, who calls out prices for different commodities, observes desired purchases and sales at those levels, and then adjusts prices until all desired purchases equal all desired sales. The only information that need be transmitted from the auctioneer to traders is the set of prices that can be incorporated into their decentralized, decision-making processes. While it may take many iterations for such a mechanism to work (i.e., all markets to clear), individual traders do not need to know the preferences, technological options, or level of resources of other traders to make their own market plans. In modern markets with a well-functioning price system, the auctioneer is effectively replaced by many accessible retail outlets and low search costs.

Finally, we note that market systems are consistent with the philosophy, known as the Chicago School of Thought, to foster individual freedoms and minimize government intervention into private decision making. Thus, markets may be seen as desirable because they support a particular view of how economic and political activities should be conducted.

3

Nonmarket Exchange Structures

This chapter follows the approach described in chapter 2 to describe three exchange structures that are characterized by traditional rules that dictate the allocation of goods and services. Two of these exchange structures are derived from economic anthropology while the third is taken from sociological accounts of informal economy and self-help activity in contemporary industrial society.

We begin with the structures derived from economic anthropology, where our reading of the anthropological record yields two types of fixed-allocation exchange that can be rendered as collections of rules. These are the subsistence and prestige exchanges of primitive economies.

SUBSISTENCE EXCHANGE

Subsistence exchange structures consist of small coresidential groups that are both producers and consumers of the goods and services that circulate in the system. Such groups may be families, households, clans, manors, and so on, usually consisting of coresident extended kin (Nash, 1961). It often is the case that the group will not have a large pool from which to draw members, resulting in a high level of interrelatedness. The goods that they exchange tend to be nondurable, mainly foodstuffs, representing almost their entire income (Dalton, G., 1964). Services in subsistence groups usually consist of reciprocal exchanges of labor power for shelter construction or food production.

Subsistence economies usually are regarded as exhibiting very infrequent exchange. Certainly this is true of trade between groups. Where such trade does exist, it takes the form of direct barter in peripheral markets where small quantities of produce are exchanged in face-to-face transactions. The goods in such markets consist wholly of incidental or serendipitous surpluses that occur when producers perceive that they have exceeded their subsistence needs. Hence, the prices of goods in these peripheral markets do not stimulate increased production.

Demand for goods produced outside of the subsistence group is very uncommon and only likely in cases of extreme need for commodities that are unavailable internally (Forde and Douglas, 1956). Such goods are likely to be traditionally known commodities, and reciprocity is a critical motivation in the transactions. In other words, the rules of exchange foster immediate transactions and also the promise to continue transactions in the future. Such offers to supply are made by open display at a customary point of exchange, such as a roadside stall or a silent trade post. Silent trade occurs when exchange partners do not meet face-to-face or through an intermediary (Montandon, 1934). For example, agriculturalists may leave produce at a customary location for fishermen from another tribe to take and leave fish in exchange (Quiggin, 1949). Such exchanges may be indicative of a low level of trust between partners, particularly fears for physical safety. Even in silent trade, however, the expectation of future repetitions of exchanges reinforces transactions between groups. Even so, information remains restricted between groups and, because it can be costly to collect, asymmetries may persist over time.

It is important to distinguish these relatively uncommon trading exchanges from the daily incidence of marketless exchange that takes place within the subsistence group in accordance with continuous social obligations that are defined by custom.

Consumption of subsistence items is shared according to fixed customary rules of allocation, such as those that require certain cuts of meat to be given to specific relatives of the hunter or those that stipulate who may expect to eat at a particular woman's cooking fire. In addition to promoting intragroup reliance and reminding members of their kinship, these rules of sharing reduce risk by assuring continuous supplies of scarcer foodstuffs, especially meat or fish (Forde and Douglas, 1956).

Demand for subsistence goods is constant and signaled through the production/consumption group. Because reciprocity is usually delayed, a bid to buy may look simply like an offer to supply; that is, goods will be offered with the expectation of a return. Bids to buy or, more accurately, to consume are made when the buyer has insufficient supply of his or her own and other producer/consumers have surplus. For goods and services that are common property, bids to share in consumption are made on the basis of availability. Offers to sell or, more accurately, to supply are made usually without expectation of immediate return.

Suppliers are the same individuals as demanders within the production/consumption groups of subsistence exchange structures. Fixed rules for allocation of particular goods to particular persons may restrict supply according to kinship or the sexual division of labor, however. Supplier restrictions may be very few and simple, such as the Bushman exclusion of women from hunting (Lee, 1968). More complex rules may stipulate a hierarchy of suppliers and demanders based on obligations of gender, age, or kinship relationship.

The subsistence structure also is characterized by simple technology for production and storage. Supply is restricted by the boundaries of the production/consumption unit and its geographical range (Nash, 1964), while storage is limited to smoked, dried, and salted products, nuts and grains, and to live storage "on the hoof" that provides blood and milk for immediate use and long-term storage of meat. There may be continual availability of certain agricultural and pastoral products, however, supplies of fish and game may be erratic (Forde and Douglas, 1959). Among hunter-gatherers production is for the satisfaction of daily needs (Lee, 1969). More technologically complex societies may produce seasonally or annually but, nonetheless, they supply immediate needs.

The principal technical constraints on subsistence supply are a low level of technological development, simplicity of tools, and lack of applied science in production techniques (Nash, 1964). Institutional constraints are (1) a relatively simple division of labor; (2) difficulty in coordinating labor for large projects, such as clearing forest for agriculture or hunting large game; and (3) the internal distributive rules that constrain supply to individuals while guaranteeing minimum availability to all group members. Seasonal variation in availability of plant and animal species is a major constraint in many areas, as well as a source of uncertainty. Also, predatory raiding by other human groups or animal species may upset supply.

Property rights in subsistence exchange structures may be quite varied. However, apart from very few simple personal items, major productive resources (i.e., land and game) are likely to be either open access as in the case of hunter-gatherers or common property (mediated perhaps through a leader or chief) as in feudalism. Where there is open access to resources, property rules do not apply since entitlements for use and management are not defined effectively. Whereas the title to such things as crops and livestock usually is held by leaders of households, usufruct (i.e., the customary right of use) commonly applies to all members of the household group whose leader is recognized as the legitimate manager of the resource. In many cases, usufruct may be enlarged to include extended kin.

Transferability of property rights seldom applies to goods or services in subsistence exchange structures. This is because members of these societies are inextricably linked together in a continuing web of obligation and counterobligation. Therefore, a resource manager may not be able to alienate property that is held (explicitly or implicitly) on behalf of a household or kinship group. In a sense, all members of the group may hold a lien on property, and title transfer may only be made legitimately by consensus of the stakeholders. Legitimation of exchange is by adherence to customary rules of distribution within the production/consumption group, and by repeated exchange with the same partners outside of the group.

Property rights are usually enforced through pressure from the kinship network in the form of argument, gossip, ridicule, shaming, and ostracism. It is not possible to separate extra-market legal constraints from endogenous exchange-enforcement mechanisms in subsistence economies because exchange of goods and services is synonymous with social intercourse; no separate agency is established exclusively for the purpose of social control. In subsistence exchange, however, very few goods will be durable property. Therefore, although enforceability holds for property, not many resources will be expended to enforce this rule.

There is no general medium of exchange in the subsistence exchange structure, nor is an independent measure of value used. Indeed, no systematic tally is kept of goods exchanged routinely within the group. Transactions are enforced by the group through shame, ridicule, and ostracism.

Within the production/consumption group, information is symmetrical and free because privacy of information is very limited. Where recognized as such, externalities may be the subject of negotiation between parties to a transaction. More usually, externalities are inherent in exchanges and may be the ultimate motivation for the exchange. In other words, exchange rules may be promoted by the group because they produce positive externalities for the whole, regardless of whether or not these rules would be selected by the individual traders. For example, sharing rules for game may not produce a net benefit for a consumer who would otherwise prefer to build credit only with the better hunters in the group. However, the externality of social cohesion provided by repeated delayed exchange may be even more important for overall survival of the group than the provision of that credit to an individual. Further, the use of fixed allocation rules may benefit the group by limiting externalities arising from individuals haggling over distribution of resources. While haggling is more consistent with individual choice, it may be wasteful of resources when survival is a primary objective.

However, it is not the case that subsistence exchange systems necessarily operate at the level of marginal survival. It is important to avoid a common ethnocentric bias that equates technological and dietary simplicity with perpetual shortage and hardship. Sahlins (1972: 9) describes how the Kalahari Bushmen and the Yahgan of Tierra del Fuego enjoy " 'a kind of material plenty,' at least in the realm of everyday useful things, apart from food and water." They achieve this affluence by restricting wants to a limited range of resources that are plentiful in their environment and limiting the accumulation of possessions to those that can be carried on their persons. Such limitations on wants are by no means unique to exotic or technologically simple societies. Dennis et al. (1969) describe various methods of income leveling and restraints on conspicuous consumption among West Yorkshire coal miners in order to maintain the cohesion of the community. Societies like the Yorkshire miners and Kalahari Bushmen are the very antithesis of those that commit extensive resources to the second type of nonmarket exchange: prestige exchange.

PRESTIGE EXCHANGE

Prestige exchange consists of the ritual transfer of certain restricted items, held in high esteem by the participants. These items are almost invariably storable and are restricted, by convention, from being exchanged for subsistence type goods (Bohannan, 1959). They may, however, constitute required payments for very important services such as bridewealth payments, homicide compensation, religious and medical fees, and dispute-adjudication fees (Douglas, 1958).

Schneider (1974) disputes the separation of prestige and subsistence goods, pointing out that Africans frequently use cattle in both ways. In some cases, however, the use of the same commodity in both spheres of economic life does not vitiate the distinction between prestige and subsistence exchange structures. The meaning that people attach to a cow as they milk it may be quite different from that which they experience when they proudly display it before their peers.

Another important aspect of prestige exchange is that transactions frequently are characterized by delayed reciprocity, so that transfers of the goods and the return payment are not simultaneous. As Mauss (1925) points out, an alternating balance of running debt is a powerful way of promoting social bonds that ensure the continuation of a relationship that is instituted by the choice of a trading partner. The prestige sphere is often overtly competitive, as trading partners attempt to bankrupt one another by continuously increasing the scale of return payments that place the recipient in debt (Strathern, 1971). Hence, the prestige exchange structure represents a hybrid of traditional fixed allocations, often involving fixed scales of equivalent values rather than prices, as well as features of true market systems, such as choice of exchange partner and negotiated prices. However, the primary object of such activities is not simply financial gain but prestige through the creation and maintenance of social bonds. The prestige structure is especially relevant to our present study in that it represents the earliest manifestations of credit and of a single medium of payment for multiple goods and services (Mauss, 1925). The operation of primitive systems of credit and close substitutes for money, in the absence of centralized guarantors, may hold important lessons for the Fat of the Land and Wasteland scenarios.

Prestige exchange also may play an important role in establishing networks for long-range trade. The exchange of nonprestige gimwali goods that accompanies the transfer of prestige enhancing kula shells is one such case reported in the Trobriand islands off Papua New Guinea (Malinowski, 1922). In this example, Trobrianders making hazardous ocean voyages, ostensibly to discharge prestige obligations, use the opportunity to engage in trade of items of everyday use (Singh Uberoi, 1962).

Demands for prestige goods or services may be made by individuals who are recognized in the community as being of comparable moral worth to the supplier and having the resources to make a future return. Demanders must be of near equivalent status to suppliers in a formal or informal hierarchy that may be based on wealth, kinship, or office.

Demanders usually will have a following based on kinship (Codere, 1950), coresidence, or personal contract (Strathern, 1971). Consumption is shared within this following according to the determination of the demander, sometimes constrained by custom (Douglas, 1958), and in accordance with his own outstanding obligations to creditors both inside and outside the following. Because demand for prestige goods is for status, large balances of debt are maintained between prestations (i.e., customary offerings) based on delayed reciprocity (Strathern, 1971). Prestige goods may be both divisible and indivisible, depending largely on the level of the exchange. However, there is a strong tendency for large major prestations to be lumpy. As participants in the system pursue greater levels of prestige, the exchanges become increasingly lumpy, exposing the trader to escalating levels of risk. At very high levels, the exchange rules become very inflexible, reflecting the specificity of the exchange.

The actual number of cattle or pigs offered may be crucial, so that the whole lot cannot be regarded as divisible. Such lots may be portioned into smaller lots or combined (as is often the case with livestock) subsequent to the exchange, to pay off outstanding creditors, or for distribution to kin for safekeeping. Prestige goods may be homogeneous, as with livestock, or heterogeneous, as with the copper plates exchanged by the Kwakiutl of British Columbia in their potlatches. These coppers derive their value not from their intrinsic worth or utility but from their particular histories of past ownership by prominent individuals.

Prestige goods also are storable, either as durable items (e.g., shells in Trobriand kula exchange [Malinowski, 1922; Singh Uberoi, 1962], blankets and coppers in Kwakiutl potlatch [Codere, 1950], iron rods among the Tiv of central Nigeria [Bohannan, 1959]) or as livestock in Papua New Guinea (Strathern, 1971) and Africa (Evans-Pritchard, 1940). Storability increases prestige through extended control over resource consumption.

Demanders are also suppliers within the networks linking kinship or local groups to prominent individuals and linking groups to one another through such individuals. Supply occurs when sufficient surplus is accumulated to pay off a major creditor and increase the scale of debt. Technical constraints on prestige supply arise from timing the availability of goods provided to the supplier by his own creditors to coincide with demand. Institutional constraints include obligations to supply other partners before one who may be making loud demands and the strict specification of the types of goods obligated for particular kinds of transaction. Natural constraints include scarcity of prestige goods, breeding cycles of prestige livestock, and weather, especially in the case of long-distance exchanges such as the Trobrianders' kula. Major uncertainties facing suppliers include coordination of assembly of goods at the time appropriate for a prestation and, in the case of delayed reciprocity, doubt about the ability of a recipient to reciprocate in the future.

The title to property in the prestige exchange structure is held by the demanders/suppliers at the head of kin or local groups, who also are entitled to use and manage it. Livestock may be distributed among kin and followers for care and breeding. Use of byproducts (blood, milk, and dung) may belong to the stockkeeper but not the flesh or title. However, exclusivity does not apply because status is achieved by conspicuous consumption or display of goods. Prestations usually will be accompanied by public feasting, dancing, and celebration. The title to actual goods exchanged may belong to a group leader, but their benefits in prestige and use will be shared by the group as a whole. Some of the costs of putting a prestation together may fall on followers who do not receive direct benefits or explicit compensation.

The transferability of property rights may apply, as with the Kwakiutl who are able to destroy copper plates and other valuables in demonstrations of conspicuous consumption (Codere, 1950). In other contexts, not all rights are transferable. For example, many kinship systems reserve some rights of a lineage over its daughters who are exchanged in marriage, even where bride price is paid.

Residual property rights may persist after the title is transferred, especially when the exchange is based on delayed reciprocity. Failure of a recipient of the title to perform some future obligation may cause the title to revert to the original owner, who may also be entitled to compensation for incidental losses from its use by another. For example, a herder reclaiming cattle from an unfulfilled marriage contract might be entitled also to claim calves that would have been his had he not transferred the beast to another (Evans-Pritchard, 1951).

The enforceability of contracts is maintained through repeated transactions, and the social sanctions of shaming, ostracism, and exclusion from the prestige exchange sphere. As with subsistence economies, it is not possible to separate the extra-market enforcement mechanisms from the exchange activity, all the more so since the principal purpose of prestige exchange is the creation and maintenance of social relations through an exchange idiom.

Bids to buy are made within the kinship or local group, or within the wider circle of group leaders who have established customary patterns of exchange. The timing of bids to buy depends on the buyer knowing that the seller has resources and that sufficient time has elapsed since the buyer made an appropriate prestation to the current seller. Also, the buyer may seek to call in debts when pressed by his own creditors.

Bids to buy are made through hints and complaints recalling previous prestations from the present consumer to the present potential supplier. Recollection of existing lineage debts from previous generations may be important in bids to obtain wives. Of course, as was previously observed, not all debtors are equal.

Offers to supply may be made to a particular creditor without necessarily an expectation of immediate reciprocity. Once again, not all creditors are equal. The supplier will attempt to give priority to exchange partners with marginally higher status than his own. The timing of offers to supply are chiefly dependent on resource availability and the time elapsed since receiving a prestation from the current demander. Timing may also be affected, as among the Kwakiutl, by the need to save face or regain status lost as a result of some independent humiliation (Codere, 1950).

The media of exchange are a limited range of customarily recognized prestige goods. These include (in various places) women, cattle, pigs, shells, iron rods, raffia cloth, and coppers. Some of these commodities may become close substitutes for money in the prestige sphere and are used for bridewealth and mortuary payments, initiation fees to various cults, homicide compensation, court fees for dispute settlement, and so forth. Subsistence goods, however, are not accepted in exchange for prestige goods in any quantities except in exceptional circumstances defined by ritual obligation or extreme emergency need (Douglas, 1958; Bohannan, 1959). Pricing in prestige spheres is almost invariably according to convention or arrived at through haggling around conventional norms or ideals.

Just as transactions are legitimated through feasting or another public celebration usually involving conspicuous display or consumption, they are enforced through shaming. Defaulters may be "rubbished" or excluded from future transactions with any partner (Strathern, 1971). Legalistic sanctions also may be applied, but these seldom are entirely separate given the multicentric nature of exchange.

Participants in prestige exchange try to restrict accurate information about their resources in order to defer the demands of creditors. However, this usually is difficult in small-scale societies. As in the fine-art market and the desirability of acquiring English stately homes, information about the good, the demander, and the supplier is an integral part of the prestige exchange structure. This is caused by the fact that prestige exchanges are characterized by general display.

Where information costs are low, it is likely that the history of the good, its past owners, and its new owner will affect the level of prestige that is attached to the trading of the good. An English home that is known to have been occupied by an historical personage or family derives value from the personal prestige of its former owners. A work of art that has been displayed in several major museums is likely to sell for more than a technically comparable piece by the same artist that has remained in obscure ownership for many years. In such cases, prices for prestige goods are used as screening devices but do not necessarily reflect immediate demand/supply information. Similarly, a Rolls-Royce or a designer garment carries a price that does not merely reflect demand for luxury cars or clothing. Where information costs are high, perhaps because there are many traders, the price of the good is more likely to be used as a measure of its prestige value. Within conventional limits, prices will be responsive to characteristics of current and past traders for the good, especially where it is difficult to determine the precise quality of the good.

It is almost perverse to talk of correcting externalities in an exchange system that exists primarily to generate effects that would be considered externalities in conventional or, as we call them elsewhere, formal market systems. Prestige exchanges invariably benefit more persons than the immediate parties to the exchange, for without public display exchange that is designed to confer or obtain status or social recognition and promote social bonding and loyalty to kinship or local groups would become meaningless. At the very least, others will be invited to a feast or party to witness the exchange as, for example, at weddings.

Both prestige and subsistence exchange may coexist in space and time. For example, that man cannot live by bread alone is illustrated by the existence of prestige spheres in very simple subsistence societies, such as the Papua New Guinea highlanders described by Rappaport (1968) and Strathern (1971).

Each of the exchange structures derived from economic anthropology describes only the particular sphere of exchange under discussion. It is not intended to be understood as a description of the totality of the socioeconomic life of a people. The individual features of each sphere, as well as the particular interrelationships between spheres in any society, are sources of the immense variety of human organization described by ethnographers (Herskovits, 1962).

As pointed out in chapter 2, not all such combinations of subsistence and prestige activities in face-to-face societies are to be found in the exotic cultures most often studied by anthropologists. Sociological studies of contemporary urban neighborhoods show that, when excluded from the formal market economy, people often develop informal trading and exchange systems with numerous transactions of goods and services employing a variety of skills. Two exchange structures derived from sociological studies of industrial societies are considered in this book. One, considered essentially nonmarket, is described in the following section. This we have called intimate exchange. Another informal economic structure, which we refer to as associational exchange, satisfies the conditions of a true market structure; it is included in the following chapter.

INTIMATE EXCHANGE

Intimate exchange takes place within communes, cooperatives, self-help organizations, and extended family networks. The object of these exchanges is to emphasize the interdependence of network members at the same time as providing them with access to goods and services that they would be unable to obtain through conventional markets.

To be in the demand for a good or service in this exchange structure, consumers must belong to one or more specific transitive networks. In many respects, intimate exchange networks are comparable to the production/consumption groups of subsistence exchange. Members of effective networks include family, close friends, and kin. Kinship is not restricted to blood ties. As indicated by Stack's (1974) study of exchange among low-income urban blacks, intimate networks extend to socially recognized kin, encompassing friends who satisfy kinship expectations and can be relied upon to support the group. In Latin cultures this institution of pseudo-kinship is institutionalized as the compadrazgo (Gudeman, 1971; Lomnitz, 1971). Geographical proximity usually will be important for network integration (Dow, 1977).

The issue of property rights is central to understanding intimate exchange structures. The title to specific property is held by individual group members who have the right to transfer it both within and outside of the group. The entitlement to manage property held within the group is exerted by the network itself, however. Entitlement to use such property is held temporarily by any member with an expressed need, given that the resource is currently available, and not being used by someone else whose needs are collectively judged to be equivalent. Membership in the network implies that the use of the property by other members is agreed to voluntarily by the owner. Seizure by someone outside of the network is countered by extra-market legal constraints, such as appeals to the police and the court system of wider society.

Consumption within the network is shared according to the principle of positive reciprocity. The reason for such sharing is a perceived dependency on the network for day-to-day support. Principles operate that prevent any member from (1) collecting an abnormally large share of the network's resources (Lomnitz, 1971); (2) acting in direct competition with other members (Stack, 1974); and (3) being denied access to goods and services because of their diminished capacity to reciprocate, as is the case with children, handicapped, infirm, or elderly members (Lowenthal, 1975). This monitoring process is facilitated by the symmetry of information that is available within an intimate network where everyone is known to everyone else.

Demand for goods or services in the intimate exchange structure may be for survival, as in subsistence exchange, or status, as in prestige exchange. Among low-income groups, there is usually a consistent demand for survival because of the frequency of crisis events. Among high-income groups, demand may be for status or to achieve political office. The act of exchange is performed in many cases to reinforce social obligations among group members rather than when particular wants arise. "A person who values such a relationship will activate it periodically in small matters, rather than wait for a pressing need to arise; he thereby shows his friends that he is ready to be of service to them at any time" (Lomnitz, 1971: 96).

It follows from the localization of supply and demand within the network that the suppliers of goods and services are essentially the same as the demanders. This arises from the interdependence of network members and the condition that all skills, resources, and services are shared according to the expressed needs of those members (Stack, 1974). Furthermore, it is common to find that members are united by common experiences, which imply similar abilities.

Supply is highly dependent on the operation of the network including the maintenance of boundaries, optimal network sizing, the ability of the network to obtain resources from the outside market economy, and the competence/expertise of network members. The supply of services is fairly continuous as long as the network is sufficiently stable. The supply of goods, however, is highly dependent on the formal market system and usually is characterized by erratic availability.

The major uncertainty facing suppliers is resource availability from the formal markets. To some extent, this uncertainty can be mitigated by gossip channels among networks. Dow's (1977) study of urban poor found that gossip is one of the principal goods exchanged in intimate networks and that one of its functions is to convey information about resource availability. Furthermore, such information is the principal commodity exchanged by brokers or gatekeepers who belong to multiple networks that would otherwise have access only to their own information.

One way to overcome uncertainty of supply is through storage. Indeed, goods may be stored centrally within intimate networks, but particular transaction rules make it likely that this will occur only for short periods of time, if at all. It is more likely that savings will exist within the network on a group basis, where members repeatedly swap goods with each other so that there is continuous redistribution. Hence, a particular demand for durable goods may not be a final consumption. Stack (1974: 33) describes how low-income urban blacks swap durable goods with each other in order to trade them for daily necessities: "As people swap, the limited supply of finished material goods in the community is perpetually redistributed among networks of kinsmen and throughout the community."

There is more certainty about services because the network consists of a limited number of identified consumers and suppliers. Services are stored in the skills of the members, where a constant inventory level is maintained for network stability. Information about members' skills is readily available within the network, which enables people to calculate the total resources available at any time.

Bids to obtain goods or services within the network are made by expression of need in the course of daily interactions. In some cases this may be direct, while in others it may be a general expression of need, thus allowing suppliers to propose the terms of the good or service. Among the Chilean middle class, "In requesting or returning a favor certain rules of civility are observed in order to avoid mutual embarrassment. Requests for favors are intimated, suggested, or phrased as requests for advice, so that the compadre is free to propose the service on his own terms" (Lomnitz, 1971: 96). However, a fundamental aspect of the bids to buy in intimate exchange is that shopping around in the network is limited. Thus, consumers do not have the option of making comparisons across a number of suppliers because this would undermine the trust of the social relationship. Offers to supply goods and services in the intimate exchange structure are made without expectation of direct and immediate material returns. The obligation to return is left implicit in the offer. In addition, there is the principle of adequacy of response that, according to Lowenthal (1975: 462) "requires that those responding to a need do so as fully as they are able even though the person in need may not have responded to others to the same extent, owing to his own limitations."

Offers are affected by timing in one of three ways. The first is to respond to an expressed need of the consumer. In this case, the supplier attempts to fulfill completely the need of the network member. In the second case, where an expressed need is not outstanding, sellers will offer goods and services to maintain a debt balance with other network members (Davis, 1972). This debt balance is crucial to reinforce the relationship among members and ensure that it will exist for the times that there are expressed needs. Finally, offers to sell will depend on resource availability. Maintenance of debt is one way of smoothing the effects on the network from resource uncertainty. It also provides the means whereby externalities are corrected within the network. Prices for goods and services are negotiable after the transaction through evaluation and adjustment of the running debt balance. Price adjustment also is facilitated by the absence of an explicit medium of exchange, because members use a barter system.

Membership in the network is essential to both the legitimation and enforcement of transactions. Thus, members have some notion of their standing in the network and social pressure is used to make them conform to the rules of the group. These rules include the requirement that certain transactions be maintained, such as the running debt balance between traders, multi-stranded transactions, and the habitual exchange of goods and services in the absence of a needs or wants motivation. Failure to live up to norms of participation is met by moral pressure exerted through shaming and the use of mild to severe verbal aggression, irony, ridicule, and condemnation (Henry, 1983). These evaluations are constantly delivered through gossip, as shown in Mars and Altman's (1983a) study of Georgian Jewry. The pressure to comply with consumer requests occurs even at great inconvenience to the supplier (Henry, 1978). The quality of the performance is a major determinant of the supplier's standing in the network (Lomnitz, 1971).

In certain respects, the intimate exchange structure may be viewed as a hybrid of subsistence and prestige exchange. However, it is unique in that it is found within, and often opposed to, the larger economic structure of contemporary industrial society. Intimate exchange, identified in sociological studies of self-help and informal economy activities, exists as a parallel economy to the market exchange structures described in the following chapter.

CONCLUSION

We characterize all three of these exchange structures as nonmarket types of exchange because of certain shared features. Most obvious is the absence of money or a close substitute to act as a universal, independent medium of exchange, unit, and store of value. Certainly, in prestige and intimate exchange networks participants make judgments about equivalent values of different commodities. These even may be standardized within a system. Even in the prestige exchange structure, however, there is no one item that is universally exchangeable.

The absence of money should not be interpreted as a failure of nonmarket exchange structures. In fact, the absence of money facilitates an important function of such systems, which is to promote the solidarity of social networks. The absence of a universal medium of accounting forces participants to keep very specific tallies of the equivalencies of commodities and services that they give and receive within the network. Whereas the primary emphasis of market accounting systems is on the quantity of profit or loss, for these nonmarket systems the identity of debtors and creditors is possibly more important than the quantity of credit or debt.

Strong emphasis on the maintenance of collectivity within social networks seems to contrast starkly with the ideal of economic individualism that stands at the center of conventional economics. Indeed, development economists have suggested that the extended kinship systems of Africa and Asia are an unsuitable basis for economic growth because economic individualism is a necessary condition for economic progress (Belshaw, 1965). Paradoxically, the success of Asian families in trade in the United States seems to rely on their ability to call on extended family networks to supply labor and capital. These family networks, keys to success in the market, rely on nonmarket exchange for their existence and durability.

Conventionally, development economists view traditional obligations as a major obstacle to "getting the prices right" in developing economies and, therefore, seek to eliminate nonmarket systems from the economic landscape. Despite such efforts, nonmarket exchange remains a durable feature of the economies of both developing and developed countries.

Despite the absence of money and the concomitant problem of nonmarket exchanges for price theory, however, our approach of specifying the rules constituting an exchange structure emphasizes the continuity between nonmarket and market exchange structures. In the future, an approach such as ours may help development economists to build upon traditional systems of exchange to promote economic growth rather than see such systems merely as millstones to development.

4

Market Exchange Structures

This chapter follows the same format as the preceding one in discussing the rules for exchange structures. The rules of the exchange structures that we present here, however, imply a different allocational outcome and fulfill, in various degrees, the conditions constituting a market process.

In directing production and distribution, market exchange structures do not rely on fixed-allocation rules arising from custom or command. Rather, these exchange structures rely on rules that are more responsive to the desires of traders engaged in the transactions for goods and services. In addition, the rules of the market exchange structures allow a good deal of choice over transaction options. As a result, current demand and supply conditions have a much greater influence in market structures than nonmarket exchange structures.

The market exchange structures discussed in this chapter span a broad range of exchange activities. The peasant marketplace (from economic anthropology) and associational markets (derived from the informal economy literature) are followed by the neoclassical economic model of the perfectly competitive market and the extreme example of the absence of competition, the monopoly market. The characteristics of perfect competition and monopoly can be considered as two extremes of the formal market spectrum. We also describe several other variations of imperfectly competitive markets insofar as their rules vary from those of monopoly markets.

THE PEASANT MARKETPLACE

The peasant marketplace consists of persons who produce for trade, usually in localized marketplaces (Dalton, G., 1964). Despite this difference from subsistence exchange, the contrast between peasant and subsistence production is largely institutional and economic rather than technical. For example, where both are based on agriculture, they are likely to use small family-managed land allocations and similar agricultural technologies. Where both are based on pastoralism, peasant producers and subsistence producers are likely to exploit open-access grazing rights.

The technology and applied science available to peasant farmers and pastoralists may be indistinguishable, in some cases, from that available to the subsistence producer (Nash, 1964). The contrast is that unlike the subsistence structure, with its emphasis on self-sufficiency and isolation, peasant producers are outward looking, seeking to produce for trade, often with urban populations who will provide the peasant producer with manufactured goods or money (Firth, 1951).

Anyone entering the marketplace with goods to exchange or money to purchase may be the source of demand. Differential transportation costs, however, may constrain entry unless rotating mechanisms are used, for example, shifting the location each day on a weekly cycle (Nash, 1964). Demand is principally for survival or to benefit from differential skills or preferences. In some cases peasant-market producers specialize to the exclusion of maintaining their own subsistence and rely exclusively on the market trade for other goods (Lewis, 1951). Consumption is shared at the discretion of the buyer, usually within a co-resident extended family.

The goods and services traded in the peasant marketplace may be divisible or indivisible, homogeneous or differentiated. Most agricultural goods are homogeneous, but limited manufactured goods may be traded. However, most trade is for agricultural products, fish, pastoral products, and so on, which are produced on peasant smallholdings. The supply of such goods tends to be highly seasonal, depending to some extent on climate and location. Purchase of large, predominantly non-seasonal items may be lumpy—for example, land. Generally, storage is limited to salted, dried, or smoked products, or live storage on the hoof. Incentives to store may depend on the extent of the seasonal variation.

Suppliers are admitted to the peasant marketplace on the same basis as demanders. However, suppliers may prefer to deal with regular customers with whom personal ties reduce risk (Mintz, 1961). Offers to sell are made by displaying goods in the marketplace.

Technical constraints on supply include the simplicity of hand tools, a low level of technological sophistication, and reliance on human labor, which is inexpensive relative to other resources of production. Institutional constraints include the nature of land-tenure patterns and rules, inheritance rules, especially for land and cattle rights, a low level of division of labor, and problems of mobilizing human labor for large projects such as irrigation or bridge construction. Natural constraints include seasonal variation, weather conditions, and soil quality. The availability or proximity of raw materials for specialist activities such as blacksmithing, potting, and medical services also constrain supply. Major uncertainties to suppliers are seasonal or weather variations, and health effects on labor resources.

The supplier in the peasant marketplace holds the title to produce but may or may not hold title to land. In such cases of usufruct, the landowner may have title over various portions of the produce. As in subsistence economies, land actually may be a common resource (Scott, 1976), privately managed, with the landowner, or village chieftain responsible for the allocation of managers. Otherwise, the entitlement to use and manage property belongs to the peasant farmer (head of household), and the condition of exclusivity applies insofar as goods and services are treated as private property.

Likewise, the transferability of property is maintained, except for land. Severance rituals to break the social bond between beast and master may be invoked in transference of livestock from one owner to another (Mauss, 1925). Bids to buy in the peasant marketplace are made by inquiry about the asking price to a producer/vendor as a basis for haggling. The location of such bids depends on the goods or services but principally will be made at a customary marketplace. The timing of bids to buy is determined at regular intervals established by custom, for example, at daily or weekly markets and seasonal fairs (Bohannan and Dalton, 1962).

The medium of exchange in peasant marketplaces may be cash or barter. The object of exchange is usually for a direct monetary equivalent. Transactions are characterized by haggling both before and after repeat exchanges. Haggling is pervasive in this market structure, possibly because time is a relatively less expensive resource than other resources. Moreover, the face-to-face (nonanonymous) nature of the exchange forces traders to negotiate their conflicting objectives. The conflict stems from the condition that the single seller is a monopolist (at least for a single contemplated transaction) and the single buyer is a monopsonist (again, for this single transaction), and neither of them is a price-taker. The balance in their market power implies that this is a situation of bilateral monopoly. In such a situation, the negotiated price will be lower than the price preferred by the monopolist and higher than the price preferred by the monopsonist.

Transactions are legitimated by handshake, exchange of goods (or sometimes livestock), or a severance ritual intended to symbolize consent. Transactions are enforced through repeat exchange, the maintenance of the market peace by a political patron, or the extra-market legal system that is necessary here because the simple nature of the exchange precludes social controls through other channels.

Identifiable externalities may be negotiated between the producer of the externality and the affected party. However, it is likely that externalities go unrecognized.

THE ASSOCIATIONAL MARKET

The associational market consists of a looser-knit network than the intimate exchange structure discussed in chapter 3. The goods and services that are offered through this structure may vary over time depending on availability. Exchange here is less likely to be essential for survival than in the intimate exchange structure. Participation is usually motivated by a desire to obtain goods at a lower price than they are available for in the formal market, by a desire for status, or by a desire for goods that are unavailable in formal markets.

In describing the irregular sources of goods in associational markets, we are not referring to those that have been expropriated unwillingly from holders of legitimate property rights. We consider goods obtained in this way to be circulating in what we call the criminal variant of associational exchange. The associational market, in contrast, consists of items sold by wholesalers direct to individual consumers, goods that are taken from the workplace as "perks" with the complicity of the employer, or are produced without respect to legal requirements for weights and measures, quality, or licensing requirements. Examples of these last items would include homemade preserves and wine, home brewed beer, and certain quasi-professional services such as legal or financial advice and veterinary or medical treatment.

Demand for goods and services in the associational exchange structure is made by members of extended networks that include friends, co-workers, neighbors, acquaintances, and friends of friends. In contrast to the intimate exchange structure, associational networks are extended and, thus, members may not know each other well or even at all. To protect the network, new consumers will be tested by extensive verbal probing, and a relationship of temporary intimacy will be established prior to admittance to the network. Demanders, however, generally act on their own behalf in associational markets so formal rules for sharing are unlikely.

The goods and services traded in the associational exchange structure are predominantly differentiated. Demand for them may be prompted by a variety of motivations including status. For most goods there will be sampling; trust in trading partners, therefore, is not a constraint on demand. For other goods that are of irregular origin, nondivisible, or obtained through greater distance in the network, trust will be important to the relationship.

Suppliers, on the other hand, enter the associational market because there is unemployment or underemployment of their resources in the formal market, because they are already members of the extended network that supports it, or because there are institutional constraints in the formal market that they seek to avoid. Participants in the associational exchange structure typically see their activity, however, as either temporary or supplemental to legitimate income sources.

Bids to buy are made, at any time, on the basis of comparisons with the formal market for similar goods. Buyers are free to accept or reject any offer from the network. Offers to sell are made through the network, but, unlike the intimate exchange structure, suppliers are free to accept or reject any offer to buy. Also in contrast with intimate exchange, offers to sell are made with the expectation of equivalent and immediate material return. Goods and services are generally valued in monetary terms but money need not always be the medium of exchange. Prices are negotiable prior to consumption but not after consumption has taken place. The legitimation of exchange contracts is implied by the consent of the trading parties.

The supplier's ability to obtain goods and services from formal markets constrains the timing of offers to sell. Unlike intimate exchange, services in the associational markets are also constrained because suppliers are faced with large opportunity costs of diverting supply from the formal economy to the informal sector.

Buyers and sellers have equal control over where transactions take place for most cases. Loose network boundaries constrain the place where offers to sell are made. Similarly, the physical or geographical location of the network will affect where supply occurs but not to any great extent. The location of supply may be more severely constrained by the need to conceal goods and services from existing legitimate traders, regulators, or enforcers in the formal markets.

In fact, its dependency on the regular market economy places a wide range of constraints on the associational exchange structure. For instance, although the parasitic nature of associational exchange combines with its wider social network to make the timing of supply less erratic than in intimate exchange, its dependency and irregularity make members vulnerable to sudden breaks in supply (Mars and Nicod, 1984). Associational exchange is highly correlated with the business cycle in the formal markets and is often the first area to be cut back or scrutinized by institutions of the formal economy under poor market conditions.

Indeed, major institutional and technical constraints on supply depend on the degree of policing and security and on prices relative to the legitimate market. The type of supply also depends on the formal occupation of the supplier who is the source of the supply to the associational market (Mars, 1982). Hence, major uncertainties face suppliers concerning the state of the formal economy and changes in the level of policing. Information asymmetries exist in both demand and supply. Buyers may lack information on sellers, especially where the transaction is irregular. Sellers may lack information on the value of the goods or services to buyers because such information is costly to collect. The cost of collection will depend on how observable and how frequent are the associational transactions.

Furthermore, the informal nature of the supply implies that there are high opportunity costs for producers to store and thus storage is unlikely. In addition, to the extent that the supply is irregular, storage will be a risky activity implying that the tendency is for immediate distribution (Henry, 1978). Property rights in the associational exchange structure do not necessarily recognize those of the wider society. Inside the network, the titles to resources are held by trading agents who also are entitled to use, manage, and transfer the property. Because certain property rights are not completely shared, there may be some external effects for traders related to the associational exchange. For example, wholesale trade with a final consumer is regarded as illicit by retailers. The retailers may undertake monitoring activities or impose sanctions on the wholesaler as a result. Property rights are only enforceable through exclusion from the network or threats of retribution from members with greater market power. The exception to this is the situation in which the owner is endowed with the right of enforceability by the extra-market legal system. Similarly, contracts are enforced loosely by the recognition of opportunities for repeated exchange or competition from legitimate sources.

Within the network, externalities, to the extent that they exist, will not explicitly be adjusted. Outside the network, attempts will be made to recover losses that are caused by informal trading.

THE CRIMINAL VARIANT OF ASSOCIATIONAL EXCHANGE

The criminal variant of the associational exchange structure is that in which the goods and services that are traded have been stolen, obtained by fraud, or are defined by the extra-market legal system as illegal goods. This category includes contraband, illegal drugs, hardcore pornography, stolen property, and the services of pimps, prostitutes, and assassins. As participants in the criminal exchange structure, as opposed to simple associational exchange, most suppliers obtain the majority of their income from the criminal market. This exchange structure possesses certain restrictive rules specifically deriving from the need to avoid apprehension by society's control agents, such as private security and police or securities commissions, as well as from the organizational structure of criminal enterprises. For example, consumption of the fruits of criminal activity may be individual or shared according to the distinct hierarchy of a criminal gang.

Demand, in some cases of criminal exchange, may be for survival, status, or merely the desire to obtain something for less than its formal market cost. In all these cases, sampling of the goods will be very restricted, although there may be some opportunities for repeat exchange. Criminal suppliers are severely restricted by a system that is comparable to formal market licensing. The location of supply depends largely on the legitimate activities that are the source of goods and can occur anywhere detection by external regulators can be avoided. The timing of supply depends on the changing opportunities afforded by legitimate institutions (e.g., changing law enforcement or changing restrictions imposed by regulation of the formal markets). Storage is possible but the illegal nature of supply implies a requirement for transient supply outlets. Two major uncertainties are the possibility of getting caught and the untrustworthy sources of information.

Goods and services are always slightly differentiated, especially by differences in suppliers or the terms of negotiation. For particular goods or services, such as prostitution or stolen property, they may be highly differentiated. Bids to buy must be made under a veil of secrecy, as efforts are made to restrict information about the intention to bid. This factor, plus the nature and quantity of goods, determine where bids to buy are made. If demand is for survival, then the timing of such bids is constrained by immediate need. Otherwise, bids to buy are likely to be made very close in time to the actual exchange. Similarly, offers to sell will be linked in time to offers to bid since this reduces the risk of leaking information to others. Hence, information about the intention to supply is very restricted.

Most offers to sell will be made from transient supply outlets and are likely to be based on a fixed pricing rule. Money is the medium of exchange. Negotiation may occur prior to consumption but not after the transaction is completed, while enforcement of contracts is performed by the threat of exposure or the sanctions of the criminal corporation.

Within the criminal market private property rights prevail over exchanges. Outsiders, from whom goods were unwillingly or unwittingly obtained for introduction into the criminal market, do not recognize the internal property rights as legitimate and will attempt to regain property through the extra-market legal system when possible. This exposes "owners" to the risk of confiscation. Hence, for some illicit goods and services exclusivity is not a meaningful concept.

To the extent that the sources can be identified, there will be continual attempts to adjust for negative externalities both within the criminal market and between the criminal market and the formal economy.

PERFECT COMPETITION

While the peasant and associational structures can be considered as having a combination of traditional and market allocation rules, the formal markets respond directly to demand and supply conditions. Among the formal markets, the perfectly competitive market produces the best economic result, where all factors of production are employed up to the level that exhausts their net social benefit and all goods are traded up to a level that exhausts the net gain in consumers' utility. The result, however, relies on the complete absence of market power and uncertainty, both of which are prevalent in real-world markets. Markets that are less than perfectly competitive also respond to demand and supply conditions, but the allocational results involve waste and payments to resources above and beyond their true cost of production. To appreciate the influence of the competitive forces in the market, we present first the rules of the perfectly competitive market and then those of the monopoly market where the absence of competition among suppliers is complete.

The major characteristic of the perfectly competitive market structure is the complete absence of market power on the part of any buyer or seller. This characteristic emerges from the rules and conditions that apply to the demanders and suppliers, as well as the requirement that transactions are conducted with negligible uncertainty. Transactions conducted in a perfectly competitive market structure are distinct and divisible and occur between anonymous traders. Although no true real-world example exists of this structure, markets in Western economies for items such as shoes and clothing come close to exhibiting the rules of the perfectly competitive market structure.

There is a large number of buyers in the perfectly competitive market, such that no individual or group faces differential access to the market. For example, anyone willing to pay the price of a pair of shoes may demand them. Coalition formation among buyers is ruled out either because bargaining is costless and an allocational outcome is achieved that could have been achieved through competitive behavior (Aumann,

1964) or because bargaining is very costly, thus competitive bidding in the market is cheap (Arrow, 1969). Where it is practical to form coalitions, demanders may do so to increase their market power, a consideration that is discussed in a later section.

Consumption in the perfectly competitive market usually is limited to the individual trader. If sharing exists, it is so minor that it does not alter the allocational and distributional characteristics of the market. Similarly, consumption must be effectively divisible so that no barrier to it exists. For example, if goods are lumpy, as with housing, then demand is unlikely to be very repetitive and sampling becomes a major source of informational disparity among demanders.

No distinction is made between survival and status because it is assumed that all demand arises from wants and utility maximization. Furthermore, the large number of buyers implies that demand in the competitive market cannot be of the sort that arises out of an immediate need, unless a large number of consumers are subject to the same crisis event.

As with the demand side of the market, there is no differential access to the market imposed on sellers and no positive return to be made from coalition formation. There is easy entry and exit in the market so that producers can emerge and leave according to the price signals they receive from the market. Economists refer to this condition as the perfect mobility of resources. Restaurants in large cities are a good example of the easy entry and exit of firms in the market.

High resource mobility guarantees that supply will occur anywhere and anytime that suppliers receive an adequate price for their goods or services. There is no incentive to store goods in this structure, because there are no major uncertainties and no constraints on market entry or exit.

While there are no differential physical or technical constraints on supply, there are constraints arising from competitive behavior and profit maximization. In particular, in the short run suppliers will produce only if price covers variable costs; in the long run they will produce only if price covers average cost. Further, the competitive pressures on producer survival will drive all producers to the same long-run production conditions where all extranormal profits are eliminated. This results from the descriptive rule that goods and services are homogeneous. Because all Idaho potatoes are fairly similar, no one Idaho farmer can expect to receive a price that is substantially different from the price received by his or her neighbors.

All of the property rights in the formal markets discussed in this chapter largely follow the rules of private property. The title to property is held by individual owners or corporate entities. In general, property is allocated to the use that results in the highest production or consumption value (Umbeck, 1976). This allocational rule is actually an outcome of the private property rules where owners hold the rights to use and manage the property, owners receive all costs and benefits derived from the use of the property, and rights are both fully transferable and fully enforced by extra-market legal mechanisms.

When conducting transactions, buyers are price takers. This means that no single demander can influence price by the decision to buy. Price is accepted by the demander if it is less than or equal to the consumer's marginal valuation of the good or service. In other words, consumers buy when they feel the price is worth the satisfaction they receive from obtaining the good or service. Sellers are price takers but have control over the amount they supply to the market. The suppliers accept prices if they are greater than or equal to the incremental cost of supply and set production at the profit maximizing level of output.

The price-taking rule implies that bids to buy and offers to sell are not limited by any temporal or spatial restrictions. Traders observe a certain price in the market and can purchase or sell as much as they want at that price. Prices may change over time, but the changes occur because of the aggregate actions of the market traders. Individual actions have an insignificant impact on the market price.

In most formal markets, the price system signals the value of goods and services. In perfect competition, the price mechanism requires a costless medium of exchange (e.g., currency) to prevent the medium of exchange from imposing a restriction on market entry. In the aggregate, prices are bid up by consumers in situations of excess demand and bid down by suppliers in cases of excess supply. Consumers and producers can respond immediately to the price signal and adjust their quantity decisions.

An alternative mechanism, which could be implemented through a computer network, is a costless bidding system where the plans of buyers and sellers are reconciled by their responses to announced prices (Smith, 1986). After collecting the information on excess demand and supply from the two groups, the auctioneer continues announcing prices until the market clears exactly. Trading may not be allowed outside of this process. In this case, money is not a necessary condition (the price of a good relative to some other good may be used), but if money is not used the transaction costs of completing the exchange must be negligible.

Transactions in the perfectly competitive market are legitimated through consent of trading partners subject to the rules of the extra-market legal and regulatory system. Transactions are enforced by repetitive transactions and competition from alternative buyers and sellers. Because information is freely available and symmetrical, externalities do not exist that have not been eliminated already by costless negotiation.

The descriptive rules of the perfectly competitive market restrict market power on both the demand and supply side of the market. Because the salient rules and features in the monopoly, imperfectly competitive, and oligopoly markets emerge from the existence of market power on the supply side, rules that refer to demand are essentially the same as in the perfectly competitive model. In the following discussion of the supply side rules of these exchange structures we conform to the standard economic convention of assuming that perfect competition holds on the demand side of the market. Following the oligopoly discussion, this assumption is relaxed, and we explore countervailing market power for the consumers.

We also point out that the rules are based on the unregulated characteristics of the formal market structures. Regulation, generally undertaken to correct for market failure to achieve desired results or the retention of market power, will alter the rules that would emerge if market agents were left to operate on their own. Thus, government creation of a regulated monopolist or industry licensing by regulatory institutions are extra-market constraints that have obvious implications for the selected rules but do not emerge directly from the underlying conditions and assumptions regarding market activity.

THE MONOPOLY MARKET

In the pure monopoly market there is one and only one supplier of the good and service with no close substitutes available. As is the case with the perfectly competitive market, it is difficult to find many real-world examples of a pure monopoly; however, monopoly markets effectively may exist within localized economies where close substitutes for some goods are expensive to obtain because of high transportation costs. In Western economies, certain entertainers, artists, scientists, or athletes may also be considered as monopolists in the sale of their skills.

Internationally, examples of monopolies are found where state-owned firms are protected from domestic competition. In addition, some countries do not impose antitrust regulations on domestic private firms, thus, natural resource monopolies may be quite persistent over time (e.g., the DeBeers diamond monopoly in South Africa). In the United States, formal antitrust legislation has existed since 1890 with the passage of the Sherman Act, which made it illegal for a firm to monopolize trade or commerce in several states or countries. The landmark application of the Sherman Act occurred in 1911 when the Supreme Court found Standard Oil of New Jersey guilty of monopolizing the petroleum-refining industry and ordered that the company be dissolved (Scherer, 1970).[1]

A possible reason a monopoly may arise is the unique location of some input to production. Further, the timing of supply may be affected by the supply of inputs or resource uncertainty. Generally, a unique product is being considered. If the monopolist supplies more than one type of good and is a monopolist in each, then more than one monopoly market exists. The key to the monopoly position of the seller is the ability to prevent the emergence of rivals. Given the possibility of profitable trade, other potential suppliers must perceive some barrier to entry in the market. This barrier may be technical (e.g., economies of scale), erected by other institutions (e.g., a supply critical to national security), or created by property rights (e.g., owning the only source of an input). Control over the critical resources for the production process or complete and exclusive knowledge of that process are potential ways for a monopolist to eliminate the possibility of rivalry.

Where storage of the good or service is possible, this practice may be highly profitable depending on the monopolist's expectations of the future. This would be especially true where current production is cheap and the monopolist expects a significant increase in the demand for the good in future periods.

Major uncertainties are likely to be present in the monopoly market. In particular, the duration of the monopoly is highly uncertain in the face of regulation, technical change, and changing demand conditions. Monopoly behavior can be regulated by the threat of competition, even where it does not exist presently (Baumol et al., 1982).

Private property rules apply in the monopoly market as in the perfectly competitive market. The only distinguishing consideration in the monopoly market involves the exclusivity rule. Monopoly pricing behavior will cause a reduction in allocational efficiency in comparison to the competitive conditions. This implies that some resources will not be employed in their highest valued uses across all markets. Thus, there are social costs involved in the monopoly management of resources that will not be incurred by the monopoly owner (Shepard, 1979).

The rules under which bids to buy are made may be dictated by the monopolist because consumers will be price takers and the monopolist may discriminate among different consumers. With price discrimination, consumers are separated into groups according to how much they value the good. The group that values it the most will be charged the highest price. Price declines as the groups' valuations decline. Price discrimination, however, requires that resale is not possible among the discriminated groups (Henderson and Quandt, 1971). Otherwise, the group that obtained the good for the lowest price could try to compete with the monopolist and sell to groups with higher valuation levels.

Offers to sell may be according to customer classes if the monopolist discriminates. In general, the monopolist will restrict the quantity available in the market at the level where the change in total revenue (marginal revenue) just equals the change in total costs (marginal costs) for producing one more unit of the good to maximize profits. Unlike the perfectly competitive supplier who cannot set price, the monopolist may maximize profits by setting either the price or the output. Setting one will determine the other, however.

Crémer (1984) argues that the monopolist may initially offer nonprice incentives to attract customers and establish the market. Once established, the monopolist can remove the incentives and exploit the monopoly position. Establishing market power by the monopolist allows the seller more control over when and where offers to sell are made because buyers lack any significant bargaining power.

While goods are priced by the monopolist, demand must be noted in order to maximize profits. However, negotiation of prices is ruled out because buyers have essentially no market power. The monopolist recognizes that each increase in supply can be absorbed by demand only at a lower price (i.e., demand varies inversely with price). A uniform pricing rule (no price discrimination) will cause the price to fall for each increase in supply if the supply is to be fully absorbed by the demand. Under these conditions, the monopolist is aware of an additional cost of increasing output; a cost that is over and above the production cost of the good. Consequently, the monopolist restricts the level supplied to the market to reflect this additional cost. The cost is additional in the sense that a perfectly competitive supplier would not recognize it, and, therefore, total industry output would have been greater and price would have been lower under pure competition. At the restricted, monopoly level of supply, the total revenues exceed total cost of production by an amount economists call monopoly rent.

Transactions in the monopoly market are legitimated by consent of the traders subject to the rules of the extra-market legal and regulatory system. The monopolist can enforce transactions by threatening to withdraw supply.

Being the sole source of supply, the monopolist can observe very precise information on consumers' valuations of the good or service. On the other hand, information regarding the production process of the inputs to production is likely to be very restricted in order to protect the monopoly position. As a result, there are significant asymmetries in information in the market. Coupled with the severe inequality in market power, externalities are likely to be absorbed by consumers.

The imperfectly competitive and oligopoly markets also involve market power on the part of suppliers, albeit to a much lesser degree than with pure monopoly. Although the imperfectly competitive and oligopoly structures are considered to be the most representative of actual U.S. markets (Shepard, 1979), analysis of these structures is difficult because the combination of competition and market power renders some of the rules ambiguous.

Further, it has been long recognized that producers engage in activities that reduce the level of competition in their industries (Tollison, 1982). The reasons they do this, however, is a matter of debate. One side has argued that firms integrate either horizontally or vertically to increase their market power and thus, their profitability. The source of this profit is not from better ideas or better products, however, but rather through the restriction of output and the increase in prices (Bain, 1968).

The other side of the argument claims that market concentration and control of inputs and outputs of production is undertaken to respond to transaction costs. These costs may arise from (1) trying to discover prices in the direct and separate pricing of activities (Coase, 1937; Cheung, 1983); (2) insufficient market for risk reduction especially with respect to assuring an input or output market (Williamson, 1975); (3) indivisibilities in activities such as research and development (Stiglitz, 1986); and (4) as responses to the risks implied by asymmetries in information, especially with respect to quality (Barzel, 1982) or effort (Stiglitz, 1974). Many of the same explanations are useful in understanding coalition formation (attempts to increase market power) on the demand side of the market.

IMPERFECT COMPETITION

Imperfect competition resembles perfect competition in that the number of sellers is sufficiently large so that no one firm has substantial market power at the industry level. In addition, products are differentiated slightly. Each supplier offers some special feature that makes its product different, but the overall function of the products in any one industry is the same. Suppliers may compete on the basis of quality (or at least the perception of it), research and development activities, and nonprice incentives offered to consumers.

When and where the generic supply occurs are not constrained because there is easy entry and exit of suppliers (i.e., free mobility of resources). This may not be true, however, for any particular supplier. Each supplier enjoys some attribute that makes it different from its rivals. The time and place of trade may be this attribute. For example, in the U.S. economy shampoo is readily available in most drug stores, but certain shampoos are sold only through hair salons.

In the imperfectly competitive market, there are no significant constraints on the industry as a whole, but there may be technical or institutional constraints on individual suppliers such that no two are identical. Each breakfast cereal contains some special ingredient to distinguish it from competitors. Where it is difficult to prevent other firms from duplicating a production process, firms seek institutional restrictions on market entry, such as patents and trademarks.

The extreme competition among firms has a number of implications for supply rules. Supply may be storable but returns will be limited to a level that just covers cost. The objective is to keep an inventory that allows the supplier to respond quickly to changes in demand, but the likelihood of capturing a large portion of any increase in demand is small. The major uncertainty facing suppliers is their ability to retain their small market shares. Thus, they may actively seek established trading relationships with consumers. In addition, advertising will be used to distinguish a firm's product as well as signal its presence to potential customers.

Individual suppliers face their own unique set of demanders, like the monopolist, but the existence of many close substitutes implies that demand will be very responsive to changes in the imperfect competitor's prices (Chamberlin, 1956). Furthermore, in the long run, extranormal profits will be competed away by new suppliers entering the market (although their products also are differentiated slightly).

Suppliers offer to sell when marginal revenue exceeds or equals marginal costs, however, this rule may be violated when they are trying to establish greater market shares. The pricing strategy of the imperfectly competitive firm differs substantially from that of the monopolist because in the long run, the imperfect competitor will be forced to supply at a level where total costs are just being covered by total revenue. This level, however, will always imply that there is excess capacity for each supplier (i.e., they are not operating their production process at the level of lowest costs). This is one of the major inefficiencies associated with imperfect competition. Each imperfectly competitive producer uses the pricing rule of a minimonopolist where the output level is less than a perfectly competitive supplier, but as soon as extranormal profits are observed new rivals enter the market and compete the excess profits away. As a result, there are too many firms in the market and price for the generic good is higher than it would have been under perfect competition (Margolis, 1985).

Prices are not negotiated directly between buyers and sellers because of the limited market power. Although sellers attempt to set prices, realistically they can control only a narrow range of price due to the high level of competition in the industry. The need to distinguish themselves from competitors may imply that a good deal of resources flow to advertising. Kirzner (1973) argues that this is actually a beneficial aspect of the imperfectly competitive market, but others see it as a wasteful use of resources (Bain, 1968).

Transactions are enforced by the existence of repetitive demand and the presence of competition from other suppliers. On the demand side, because all products have some distinguishing feature, there is limited enforcement implied by the threat of withdrawing the supply. Because there are no major uncertainties to act as a barrier to entry, there is limited asymmetry in information about the uniqueness of the product. Firms, however, may actively pursue exclusive research and development projects to increase their relative market share.

Imperfectly competitive market structures imply some inefficiency in the economy. The costs of this inefficiency will be absorbed by the economy in the absence of regulation. On the other hand, imperfectly competitive markets adjust quickly to changes in market conditions and, therefore, provide some economic stabilization.

OLIGOPOLY

The distinguishing feature in the oligopoly market is that either there are only a few suppliers in the industry or a large segment of the market is dominated by a few large suppliers. The product supplied may be differentiated, as in the case of pharmaceuticals, or homogeneous, as in the case of rail-freight service.

Some constraint exists on market entry or exit that generates an environment susceptible to control by a small number of firms. Generally, this will arise from economies of scale or mergers in the industry. These mergers can be among firms producing the same generic product (horizontal integration) or among firms that produce related input and output products (vertical integration).

The major uncertainty facing the oligopolist is the reactions of its rivals to price and output changes. As found in the imperfectly competitive market, maintaining market share is an important concern for the oligopolistic supplier. There may be particular uncertainties, such as technological risk, or uncertain rewards for innovations that cause oligopoly to be a necessary type of market structure. In these cases, a more competitive structure is inconsistent with the undertaking of large risks (Schumpeter, 1942).

Because there are no generally accepted behavioral assumptions for oligopolistic behavior, there are numerous solutions for the pricing rules under this market structure (Henderson and Quandt, 1971). The rules presented here vary largely on the basis of assumptions regarding the oligopolist's perception of the actions of its rivals. Under one rule, the oligopolist sets its price according to a reaction function that depends on its own cost conditions, the market demand, and the output of its rivals. To construct this relationship, the oligopolist assumes that its own action will not alter the output of its rivals (i.e., there is no interdependence in the industry). Thus, the oligopolist considers the profit-maximizing level of its own output for each possible level of output of its rivals. It selects a particular level by observing the level forthcoming from its rivals. Of course, this action is likely to lead to a change in its rivals' output level, given that they have their own reaction functions, which will cause the oligopolist to select another level. Market stability can be established when there is no longer an incentive for any supplier to change output.

Using a collusive rule, oligopolists may recognize their mutual interdependence and act in unison to maximize the total profit in the industry. If one of the oligopolists believes that each of its rivals will hold production constant, however, there will always be an incentive to cheat. This implies that collusion solutions are unstable in the absence of monitoring and policing agreements by the colluders (Varian, 1978).

As another alternative, oligopolists may allow one supplier to be the price leader (i.e., rivals will mimic whatever the leader does with respect to price). This will result in a pricing outcome similar to pure monopoly.

Finally, the oligopolist may face two effective demand environments because of the reactions of its rivals. The first applies to price increases where rivals keep their prices constant and, thus, increase their market shares relative to the supplier that raises price. The second applies to price decreases where rivals follow suit to retain their relative market shares. Such a situation generally implies that the most profitable pricing policy for the oligopolist is not to change prices unless there is some significant change in its cost conditions.

Whatever pricing rule is used, the oligopolist can continue to earn extranormal profits in the long run like the monopolist. Although there can be significant competition from rival firms, rivalry does not approach the level of competition found in the imperfectly competitive markets. Legitimation of transactions is performed largely by consent between consumers and suppliers. Among suppliers, there may be conditions as part of a collusion agreement or cartel. Transaction agreements with demanders can be enforced by the threat of withdrawing the supply. On the supply side, transactions are enforced by the presence of rivals. Again, among suppliers there may be sanctions imposed by a cartel.

Because of the significant market power enjoyed by the oligopolists, information is likely to be asymmetric between suppliers and consumers. Among suppliers that act as rivals this will also be the case. If suppliers collude, then information may be shared symmetrically.

LESS THAN PERFECT COMPETITION AMONG MARKET CONSUMERS

The behavior of product demanders endowed with varying degrees of market power is analogous to that of the supply models previously presented. In fact, economists use the term oligopsonist and monopsonist to refer to few and single buyers, respectively. Because of the similarities, it is not necessary to repeat all of the rules already outlined.

Instead, we present the salient implications of market power on the demand side.

In the case of a single buyer facing a competitive supply, the entire industry supply curve becomes the relevant information for the purchase decision. Like the monopolist, who recognizes that increases in supply lead to a fall in the price received because industry demand varies inversely with price, the monopsonist recognizes that, generally, industry supply levels increase only with increases in price. From the monopsonist's point of view, each additional unit that is purchased implies a slightly higher price than the last unit. Furthermore, if the monopsonist cannot discriminate among suppliers (i.e., it must pay a uniform price for all purchased quantities of the good or service), then the average cost of its purchases will be increasing with increases in the quantity purchased. Thus, for the nondiscriminating monopsonist, price is determined by its level of demand. The higher the level, the higher the price it will pay for all units of the good or service. This leads the profit maximizing monopsonist to purchase a lower quantity of the good or service than would be purchased if perfect competition existed on the demand side. When a monopsonist faces a monopolist on the supply side, then their market powers are balanced and to some extent this may force them to collude and achieve competitive market conditions (Henderson and Quandt, 1971).

Market power that is concentrated in a few buyers facing a competitive supply will lead to oligopsonistic behavior. As in the oligopolistic market structure, there is no single solution to this problem, however. Oligopsonists may either recognize or not recognize their interdependence, collude or fight each other. In any case, there will be some market effects in that quantities purchased and prices paid will be lower than under the competitive conditions unless supply is also characterized by market power.

LINKING MARKET AND NONMARKET EXCHANGE STRUCTURES

The exchange structures presented in this and the previous chapter cover a wide spectrum of exchange activities. The applicability of each exchange structure in a particular economic environment depends on whether or not the rules of the structure are consistent with the conditions of the environment. In some environments, the rules of an exchange structure may be highly improbable or unstable. In addition, exchange structures rarely exist in isolation, so the interdependent effects between structures are also important in assessing the applicability of the structure.

Having described the various types of exchange structures in isolation, it is worth considering here Lasch's (1977) point concerning the inter-relationship between market and nonmarket structures. Nonmarket exchange (through, for example, intimate exchange structures) provided under the institutions of family and kin creates the psychological conditions of security that free persons require to operate as individuals in a depersonalized, market economy. At the same time, as Blau's (1964) exchange theory points out, the very balance and stability of the reciprocal exchange characterizing nonmarket exchange structures involves costs of foregone alternative (and quite possibly larger) rewards from participation in a market structure.

In the next chapter, we will argue that even where institutional and resource conditions support the rules of market exchange structures (e.g., the conditions of Western economies), participation in nonmarket structures persists at least for security and affiliation benefits. On the other hand, participation in these markets will never substitute for market participation completely, because for many transactions the network benefits become swamped by the costs of forgoing market efficiencies or avoiding detection. What is important for our scenario analyses to follow is that the reader appreciate that even in highly developed societies, strong links between the market and nonmarket exchange structures emerge from the interdependence of formal and informal economic activities.

NOTE

1. However, the existence of such an act did not prevent numerous attempts to circumvent it as is evinced by the numerous laws designed to address its loopholes, such as the Clayton Act of 1914, the Robinson-Patman Act of 1930, and Celler-Kefauver Act of 1950. Indeed, as Coleman (1989) points out, three of the biggest waves of mergers in U.S. history came immediately after the passage of legislation designed to prevent such monopolistic combinations. Thus, we should not overlook the efficacy of the enforcement efforts for these restrictions on transaction options.

5

Business as Usual

In the previous chapter, we used an interdisciplinary, rules-based analytical framework to take a nonconventional look at exchange structures characteristic of Western and Third World societies. In this chapter, we will examine the first of four scenarios that vary according to high and low levels of institutional and resource conditions. The conditions of this scenario correspond to a localized development or recovery problem in an otherwise highly developed economy. Such a scenario might be consistent with long-term economic neglect of a region, some inner city conditions, limited war or environmental damage, civil war effects, or shifts from highly regulated transactions to market organization in an industrialized country.

The *Business as Usual* scenario for economic development or recovery is that in which institutions and resources exist at abundant levels. Although localized problems may be extensive, the primary institutions of government and finance operate in recognizable form. The baseline for this scenario is the contemporary U.S. economy because it represents high levels of institutional and resource development. The Business as Usual scenario retains the diversity of nonmarket and market structures exhibited by the existing economy. All of the exchange structures discussed in chapters 3 and 4 are found in various degrees in the U.S. economy, although subsistence and peasant marketplaces play only a limited role.

To examine market making issues in Business as Usual, we must consider two problems. First is the creation of markets for exchange where previously some other form of social organization allocated resources. Examples in recent U.S. experience include the deregulation of the airline and natural gas markets and the increased use of marketable permits for environmental resources. The second problem that we must consider in Business as Usual is a recovery effort within a local area following a significant loss of local institutions or resources. Examples of this type of problem include natural disasters or localized financial catastrophes.

We will begin this discussion by considering the extent to which available exchange structures and formal institutions perform the basic functions described in chapter 1 as constituting the exchange activity. This discussion is key to the analysis in later chapters because it sets the baseline for comparison as we examine alternative assumptions regarding low levels of institutions or resources or both.

BASIC FUNCTIONS IN BUSINESS AS USUAL

We consider the role taken by the formal extra-market institutions in the United States in performing the basic exchange functions, and then examine the role of particular exchange structures. Two questions arise: which market structures alone are sufficient to generate what we commonly regard as business as usual in a highly developed economy and which structures rely heavily on extra-market institutions to function at all. As each function is examined, we consider the extent to which the function is performed by the exchange structure and is unimpeded by additional extra-market regulations.

Define Property Rights

In the Business as Usual scenario, property rights are defined by laws rooted in custom (such as common law) or enacted through legislation. Certain property is governed by common property rules, such as transportation routes or public parks, but most property is subject to the rules of private property. Ownership is legitimated through possession by documents proving legitimate acquisition (receipts), or by registration with a regulatory or governing authority, such as county clerks in the United States or the National Land Registry in Britain. Clearly, however, the concept of property implies that rights of ownership must be protected. This in turn implies some authority that in the United States is provided by independent courts supported by state and federal enforcement agencies. This situation contrasts starkly to that in Socialist societies where property is substantially owned by the state and protected directly by centralized state authority, as we shall see in the Bureaucratic Nightmare scenario.

In the United States, only the intimate exchange structure—and the criminal variant of the associational market—can be said to include rules that explicitly define property rights in a way that does not rely on the extra-market legal system. In the case of intimate exchange, property rights are defined through the conditions imposed on the membership with respect to the right to use and manage. In the case of criminal exchange, property rights are defined by the legal definition of wrongful possession. Formal markets take property rights as given from the extra-market legal system; however, they may define the means by which property can be transferred, as with any good that can be exchanged. Furthermore, these markets can affect the distribution of property rights because the value of these rights is usually a market outcome.

Convey Supply and Demand Information

General economic information is conveyed through formally constituted mechanisms such as stock and commodity exchanges. These institutional channels of information are supplemented by the news media, government agencies and publications, and the advertising media. Some formally established associations, such as consumer groups and mutual aid associations, also have their own networks of information distribution.

The market structures that we define as intimate, associational, perfect competition, and imperfect competition fulfill this function of conveying information to meet the desires of their trading agents through internal, dynamic mechanisms. Information is transferred quite frequently and uniformly through either network rules underlying face-to-face interactions or the price signal. As market power becomes more concentrated in the less-competitive structures, traders may establish rules that reduce the flow of information in order to retain secrecy and to limit the entry of potential competitors in the market.

Provide Opportunity for Legitimate Transactions

For goods that are nonexclusive in consumption, such as public goods like police and fire protection, the function of providing opportunity is performed by local and federal government agencies. By providing these services, the agencies effectively create the opportunity for traders to purchase them in the absence of their provision by the private markets. For private goods, this function is performed largely by the extensive network of wholesale and retail outlets in the U.S. economy. At times, government intervention is used to expand existing private opportunities by undertaking commercial activities such as the provision of electrical power (in the case of the Tennessee Valley Authority, for example) or educational services.

The rules in the formal market structures imply that increasing degrees of market power, and thus, decreasing degrees of competition, should act to limit the opportunities for legitimate transaction. In the nonmarket structures, membership is likely to be motivated by a desire to expand the opportunities for gain from exchange relative to those obtainable in outside structures.

Limit Provisions of Legitimate Contracts

In the first instance, the provisions of legitimate contracts are limited by state and federal law. Legislatures and courts outlaw exchange of certain goods and services, such as sexual services, children, or endangered species, and they limit the exchange of others, such as pharmaceuticals and explosives. Market institutions also may limit contracts, as in the case of insurance contracts, but they may rely on regulatory agencies and the courts to enforce compliance with the limitations.

In nonmarket structures, this function is performed by the rules of the network and is more likely to involve limitations on who can exchange rather than on what can be exchanged. In the case of the criminal variant of the associational market, limits are set by the rules of the criminal enterprise. In the formal markets, limitations that are additional to those of the extra-market legal and regulatory system would stem from an inequality in market power or market failure. Because of uncertainty or the presence of externalities, suppliers may be unwilling to offer a complete set of contracts to demanders because conditions are too risky or rewards do not adequately compensate suppliers for their efforts.

Enforce Contracts Other Than by Physical Coercion

The enforcement of contracts is carried out largely by the legal and regulatory systems and through the use or threat of sanctions. Administrative regulation includes prospective controls through licensing, and retrospective controls through the use of sanctions such as expulsion from the activity, through license suspension or revocation license, civil court compensation remedies, fines, and ultimately, though rarely used, imprisonment. All the exchange structures also imply some enforcement of contracts. In the less competitive markets, enforcement of contracts can be initiated by the withdrawal of payment or supply. Indeed, the nature of the enforcement ranges from social pressure exercised through the typically multidimensional relations characterizing nonmarket exchange structures (Gluckman, 1955b; Braithwaite, 1989) to monetary and penal penalties in the formal markets, which are characterized by uni-dimensional relations. However, it is important to recognize that neither system uses purely one type of enforcement system; it is customary, even in conventional business, to rely on informal means of settlement rather than the formal enforcement of contracts (Macaulay, 1963).

Settle Disputes

This function is performed largely by the state and federal court systems. Private and public mediators may also assist in the settlement process between parties in a dispute. In addition, religious institutions, regulatory agencies, and private associations often engage in dispute settlement where disputes arise among their members or between their members and outside groups.

An exchange structure may perform dispute settlement continuously where there is negotiation after consumption, as in intimate exchange, or where prices are subject to negotiation after consumption has taken place, such as formal market exchanges with continuing contractual obligations (e.g., where service provisions are included in the contract). These adjustments require that parties can be identified cheaply, however, so that negotiated compensation is possible.

Maintain Civil Order

The institutional responsibility for civil order operations resides with the state and federal lawmakers. Their decisions are enforced by the courts, police, and, in times of emergency, the military. The intimate exchange structures and criminal variant of the associational market are the only two structures with rules that do not rely almost entirely on these extra-market systems to maintain civil order among their members. In the case of intimate exchange, the network rules preclude relying on the outside system. In the case of criminal exchange, traders appear not to have the option because trading networks exist outside the protection of the formal legal system. A notable exception to this is where agreements are made for the purposes of transferring information from criminals to the police (Howson, 1970; Klockars, 1974; Henry, 1977).

Legitimate Other Functions

This function is carried out by Congress and state legislatures for the whole society, and by government agencies and the governing bodies of institutions, such as stock and commodity exchanges, corporations, and professional associations at the micro level. Courts also may legitimate other functions through their interpretations of statutes and common law.

In the market structures, enforcement and pricing are legitimated by the structure, subject to approval by whatever existing governing body oversees the transaction activities. For example, functions may be legitimated by external legal or government regulatory agencies such as the Nuclear Regulatory Commission, internal governing mechanisms such as the Executive Board of a corporation, or professional associations such as the American Medical Association. In contrast, the intimate exchange structure attempts to use its network rules and multiplex relations to legitimate other functions, thus operating like a society within a society.

Guarantee Currency and Close Substitutes

Currency is guaranteed by the U.S. government with various responsibilities falling on the Federal Reserve Bank and the Treasury for all of the exchange structures in Business as Usual. The value of close substitutes is established, but not necessarily guaranteed, by the primary market system for their exchange. The primary market and markets for authenticity activities may be internal or external to the exchange structure of interest.

Administer Distributive Justice, Including Taxation

This function is determined primarily by federal and state legislatures and by charities. Policies determined by these institutions are executed by regulatory agencies, the IRS, state and local tax officers, and charitable organizations.

The intimate exchange structure is the only structure where redistribution, over and above the formal institutional programs, is attempted by rules affecting the haves and the have-nots. In the associational, perfectly competitive, and imperfectly competitive markets, there will be a tendency to maintain the status quo because they are near the point of balanced reciprocity. In the formal markets, where market power is pervasive (e.g., monopoly and oligopoly) or the criminal variant of the associational structure, there will be a tendency to reallocate from the have-nots to the haves.

Monitor and Modify Operations in Response to Changing Circumstances

At the federal and state levels of government, this function is performed extensively to respond to the needs and demands of various constituencies. Monitoring and reporting information is a major function of many public agencies, because information is often treated as a public good. For example, the U.S. Department of Agriculture regularly monitors and reports information about changing market conditions, technology, or price expectations to reduce informational transaction costs and assist traders in modifying their operations.

In addition, all of the exchange structures perform monitoring and modification of operations independently in various degrees. In perfectly and imperfectly competitive markets, this function is accomplished by the rules fostering competition among traders. Suppliers that do not respond to changing circumstances are not likely to stay in business very long, given the price-taking position of traders and the minimal excess profit levels. In markets with greater concentrations of market power, how well this function is performed depends on suppliers' expectations regarding protection of their market shares. Where rivalry is great, suppliers are likely to invest heavily in research and development and in monitoring activities (Stiglitz, 1986). Where the threat of competition is small, the supplier is likely to ignore changing conditions and to be reluctant to modify operations.

Mitigate Risk

In Business as Usual, public and private insurance institutions are the principal institutions for mitigating risk. Regulatory controls also limit individual risks by restricting risky activities. For example, the Federal Deposit Insurance Corporation combines an insurance mechanism with regulatory controls on savings deposits to mitigate the risks of bank failures. As demonstrated by the Savings and Loan bailout, however, this process does not eliminate risk but merely distributes it widely. Society may partially mitigate risk for some groups in order to increase their willingness to take risks, such as in the limitation placed on nuclear power operators' liability under the Price-Anderson Act.

In the formal markets, risk is mitigated through an associated insurance market, by rules controlling the integration of input and output resources (for example, through mergers), or by the diversification of production or consumption activities. The intimate and associational exchange structures rely on the network rules governing mutual support and sharing to insure members against the cost of risks.

Exploit Comparative Advantage, Specialization, and Division of Labor

The formal institutions perform this function in the same way that they expand the opportunities for legitimate transactions. Encouragement of certain activities to develop a new industry, provision of information or educational programs, and interstate and interregional commerce commissions are all means of supporting the diversity of goods and services in the economy.

All of the market exchange structures exploit comparative advantage, specialization, and division of labor as responses to profit incentives. The ability of markets to exploit differences in resources results directly from the primary reliance on the rules of demand and supply conditions to allocate and distribute goods and services. The intimate exchange structure attempts to prevent specialization in labor because this goes against the consumer-as-producer philosophy. If members are too specialized their services are not interchangeable, a condition that is not consistent with the process of maintaining group cohesion.

Reduce Transaction Costs for Intertemporal or Interregional Transactions

Formal institutions perform this function by increasing the availability of credit. An example is the Federal Reserve Board's control over the money supply and the discount rate to Reserve banks to stabilize interest rates.

In the formal market structures, intertemporal and interregional transaction costs may strongly influence the sustainability of the structure. For example, firms may lower interregional transaction costs by conducting business activities through a network of wholly or partially owned subsidiaries. Such rules increase the degree of market power but decrease production costs. The intimate exchange structure reduces intertemporal costs by rules fostering delayed reciprocity, which is analogous to credit.

MISSING OR RESTRICTED MARKETS

Even in Western economies with their vast array of highly developed and functioning markets, many transactions exist that are removed from market processes. In previous chapters, we have addressed exchange structures that lack the characteristics of market processes, yet provide their members with other attributes to facilitate exchange needs. In the environment of Business as Usual, we find transactions that are excluded from market structures either explicitly by the command rules of the governing and regulatory institutions or implicitly by particular conditions that make market structures dysfunctional. A good example of the command case is the provision of public education. A good example of the dysfunctional or "missing" market case is uncontrolled pollution of air and water resources.

Economists describe missing or dysfunctional markets as *market failure*.

Market failure is strictly a condition affecting the efficiency of market results; it implies nothing for the equity of trader endowments. With Pareto-optimal market efficiency, it is impossible to reallocate resources to make anyone better off without a cost to at least one trader. The perfectly competitive market structure, however, will preserve the status quo in ownership patterns; thus, Western societies have used direct intervention in income redistribution to pursue equity goals. In the case of market failure and inefficient allocations, a policy maker can choose to intervene directly and control transaction options or to modify market rules to promote more competitive outcomes.

In chapter 4, we discussed the perfectly competitive market structure and pointed out that a key descriptive rule is that traders are price takers. This rule is satisfied by three descriptive rules of the market structure: (1) large numbers of buyers and sellers; (2) the product is homogeneous; and (3) all buyers and sellers have free and uniform access to market information and opportunities. Even in Business as Usual, these conditions are present only in a very limited number of market transactions.

A second set of rules defines the technical relationships for supply and demand and establishes the fundamental theorem of welfare economics (Debreau, 1959). A perfectly competitive market structure with particular rules governing the technical relationships generates a Pareto-optimal allocation of resources. Market failure often arises because of a violation of two particular technical rules: the absence of externalities and the presence of increasing opportunity costs.

Externalities exist where actors do not meet the full social costs of their activities (i.e., some costs are externalized). Externalities in consumption or production emerge when significant interdependencies exist among traders. For example, a consumption externality is linked with merit goods like education and technical training because all of society benefits from a well-educated work force. A production externality may be present where residual pollutants from a factory contaminate community drinking water. Externalities do not exist if all consequences of consumption and production decisions are fully reflected in the prices faced by traders.

Increasing opportunity costs in a market structure guarantees that producers have exhausted all economies of scale or economies of consolidation. Violation of this rule implies that a single large producer or a small number of producers can produce goods for less cost than many producers; therefore, we have the rules supporting the monopoly or oligopoly market structures. In these cases, producers are not price takers. Decreasing opportunity costs are characteristic of production processes where: (1) large capital (fixed investment) components are present; (2) production risks are significant; or (3) information costs are substantial.

Making Markets for Environmental Goods

A continual challenge in a political system that reveres market process and its subsequent benefits for efficiency and self-determination is how to encourage competitive market behavior while pursuing other social goals. Considering only social goals that may be in conflict on efficiency grounds, recent U.S. experience with making and improving markets provides important lessons for our consideration of Business as Usual.

In the area of U.S. environmental management, nothing less than a regulatory revolution is occurring for transactions that affect environmental and health quality. Traditionally these nonmarketed goods and services have been controlled by command regulation or, in many cases, ignored and then subjected to the tragedy of open-access property rights. In the post-Reagan era, there is growing interest at all levels of government to balance the prudent use of environmental and health resources with reductions in the regulatory burden placed on the free market system. We find evidence of this interest in the various attempts to create opportunity from adversity by offering firms and individuals incentive-based rules that make markets in environmental and health quality as alternatives to traditional regulation.

Incentive-based rules can be used to encourage efficient use of environmental resources by internalizing the consequences of traders' decisions in prices. Incentive-based rules establish the principle that the polluter pays for environmental damage to ensure economic efficiency. This principle, however, may violate the nonefficiency concern of preservationists or "deep ecologists" that pollution is a moral violation of natural rights. Three types of policy instruments can create incentive rules for traders that are specific to decisions regarding the environmental good (U.S. Department of Energy, 1989): emission fees, tradable emission rights, and deposit-refund systems.

Emission fees operate on the basis of charging an amount per unit of emitted pollutant, and thereby make producers cognizant of the environmental damage or cost of mitigation for these emissions. Under such rules, producers also face the incentive to abate the emission or invest in new research and development to eliminate it.

Using tradable emission rights, the government sets an overall level or rate of allowable emissions, and then allows firms to trade rights to contribution to the aggregate limit. Tradable emission rights create a competitive market structure for the environmental good and can ensure it will be allocated to the most highly valued uses. The initial allocation of the environmental good, however, entails many of the same equity problems as the distribution of initial endowments in more routine markets.

The deposit-refund instrument operates as an emission fee that is imposed prior to creating an emission. If the emission is avoided then the deposit is returned; otherwise, the trader has prepaid the environmental costs of the transaction.

In making markets for environmental goods, U.S. governing authorities have employed all of the incentive-based instruments already discussed. Hahn (1989) presents a case study analysis and review of some recent incentive-based initiatives. He argues that these incentives work best where one finds emission practices that are easily monitored and the goals of the environmental policy are clear to traders and are well accepted. The lead-emission trading program during the 1980s illustrates a successful use of incentive-based rules.

Other initiatives discussed by Hahn (1989) and Hahn and Noll (1983) resulted in disappointing outcomes from a market improvement perspective. In general, where the trading conditions support monopoly or oligopoly structures or where transaction costs due to uncertainty or information are high, actual experience suggests that incentive-based systems function poorly as markets instruments. The results and lessons of the newly created markets are mixed and extremely preliminary; much more experience is necessary before one can conclude that these institutional changes can accomplish their objectives.

LOCALIZED RELIEF EFFORTS

Another problem we address for Business as Usual is one where a local area has suffered major damage to its institutional or resource base, or both. Such a scenario becomes possible following natural disasters or following political or financial collapse. However, we maintain the assumption that the broader political and economic structure remains largely unchanged; therefore, this scenario captures the reconstruction or relief efforts of the larger society and the effects on the local area.

Reconstruction in the problem area may be of three kinds. First is the case where damage or decay is so great to a particular region or local area that the rest of the country decides, explicitly or implicitly, not to offer any assistance for the reconstruction of infrastructure or resources. In effect, the area will be treated as if it does not belong to the rest of the economic, legal, or political systems, and thus, restoration of social order and resource development within the area is expected to proceed along the lines of the Wasteland scenario. This is not a very likely case, however, because such neglect is inconsistent with past relief actions by developed nations and would likely be politically unacceptable to the general population.

In the second case, the outside system may restore the major institutional components, such as a legal system and agencies to enforce civil order, but decline to offer reconstruction relief in the way of sub-

sidies to reduce the cost of attracting or developing commercial resources. This case is more likely than the first, especially in the case of
a disaster that has already imposed a tremendous burden on the rest of
the economy to pay for emergency services. Where institutions are restored but resources are left largely in a devastated state, we have the
conditions for the Bureaucratic Nightmare scenario. In the Bureaucratic
Nightmare case, the stability of market structures to bring about economic recovery or development would be very dependent on the level
of conflict among local groups and the established authority.

There is, however, one important difference between the case just
described and the institution-intensive conditions of the Bureaucratic
Nightmare where resources are scarce throughout, including those that
the institutions need to maintain and enforce authority. In Business as
Usual, outside resources can, and probably would, be used in attempts
to maintain the authority of the outside system. This may not alter many
of the authority-maintenance problems. In fact, it may simply exacerbate
the social and physical damages by prolonging the period of conflict.
An example of this kind of phenomenon is the clash between law-
enforcement agencies and inner city groups (Libman-Rubenstein, 1979).

Finally, relief programs may be implemented to assist both institutional and resource development. This case would correspond to the
general pattern of U.S. relief actions following many regional and localized disasters.

Economic Relief Within the Affected Area

Hill (1987) provides an extensive review of the analyses that address
the economic recovery question from regional disasters. In general, he
finds that recovery resources do not benefit all groups equally. An understanding of the repercussions for exchange requires a distinction
between groups that are included in the relief programs and those that
are excluded.

*Exchange Structures of the Groups Included in the Recovery
Programs*

One of the more important conclusions Hill (1987) made during his
review of the literature is that once relief efforts are underway, the local
disaster produces almost no negative long-term effects on the local economy and, in fact, may result in a net positive effect. His findings support
the proposition that there is little effect on the availability of resources
once outside sources begin to augment the damaged resource base. The
following six considerations will affect exchange activities in the relief
area.

- A major source of aid to the relief area comes from an inflow of funds and technical assistance provided by federal and state agencies. Relief programs stimulate new construction of production facilities as well as an opportunity for owners of existing establishments to improve their facilities. While the inflow of funds is clearly a factor in the recovery or development success, Hill (1987) did not address the possible influence of changes in the underlying market structures.

- There are several aspects of relief programs that suggest that the rules of the dominant market structures are altered. For example, immediately following a disaster, community networks often emerge to deal with emergency and recovery activities. These community networks may enhance market power on the demand side of the market, resulting in some downward pressure on prices from countervailing market power.

- After the relief effort and the process of allocating relief funds are underway, the economic conditions may become purged of many of the inefficiencies stemming from local monopoly, oligopoly, or imperfect competition, especially in the face of long-standing supply networks. If the old rule for pricing followed a posted price (or fixed price) scheme and the new rules imply competitive bidding for relief funds, then we would expect an improvement in efficiency. Plott (1986) argues that this result can be expected where the posted price system encourages price leaders and followers.

- With relief funds and the need for new resources to undertake reconstruction activities, new firms can enter the market that are not part of the old network. Market structures should evolve with rules derived from greater competition among the suppliers, such as a move from an oligopolist structure to imperfect competition.

- Another likely change in the rules results from the lower private information costs in cases where government agencies undertake information collection and distribution activities. This not only increases the information flows within the relief area but also increases flows in the outside economic system where information is costly. Furthermore, with the greater access to funds and public agency encouragement, the risk of starting a new business in the relief area is probably reduced as well. Both greater information flows and reductions in uncertainty will be conducive to the evolution of more competitive rules.

- Resources may be removed to the informal sector by groups largely excluded from the relief program.

These six factors suggest that improved economic performance, or at least the absence of long-term economic impacts in local disaster areas within the United States, may be caused partially by changes in the underlying rules of formal and informal market structures and the inflow of disaster funds. It is puzzling, however, that these changes do not produce dramatic or permanent effects for the relief area. Two reasons why the performance improvements may be dampened are (1) the decay of the rules to less competitive structures over time and (2) the removal of some resources from the formal market structures.

First, decay of the rules to less competitive structures could result if there are real, transaction cost factors underlying the less competitive rules, as suggested by Williamson (1975) and others. These factors would begin to appear again as the relief efforts subsided and removed their beneficial influences on price setting, information, and risk. Second, the fact that not all groups will have equal access to the relief programs will encourage them to seek out other channels for their exchange activity, and they may remove their resources from the formal market structures.

Finally, it is possible that the local relief program will have no significant effect on the local economy other than perhaps causing a short-term flurry of construction activities. In other words, government intervention causes a short-term boom to the local economy, but over time this level of economic activity cannot be supported by longer term economic activity. In this case, once the subsidies are removed, there may be little permanent change in the economic performance of the area. One reason why the local economy does not sustain at least some of the gains from replacing older facilities with new facilities may be that the additional economic activity also generates additional needs for public services to support labor flows into the area. The removal of the public subsidies for development may lead to declining economic opportunities for these workers who then remain in the area and require financial assistance from local governments.

Exchange Structures of the Groups Excluded from the Relief Programs

As established in the last chapter, we actually live in a multicentric economy in which formal market structures coexist with many nonmarket structures. Studies of informal economies by researchers such as Ferman and Ferman (1973) demonstrate that modern industrial society produces conditions that provide fertile ground for this development. Ethnic and cultural distinctions and an unequal distribution of wealth and income create economic categories of people that are largely excluded from the formal economy. The formal sector fails to provide goods and services for these excluded groups at prices they can afford because it is burdened with high transaction costs including costly mechanisms for regulating standards of production and distribution. For example, economic specialization resulting from the demands of a complex technological system that requires high degrees of technical expertise, together with the growth of protectionist trade unions and professional associations, coalesce so that some goods and services are not widely available or are too expensive for large sectors of the population. These same factors exclude many people from jobs in rewarding areas of employment.

The result of these exclusions and failures is to provide a context for the emergence of a range of intimate, associational, and criminal exchange structures for low-cost or scarce goods and services. Moreover, any relief effort, while attempting to develop the foundations for economic growth, may also exacerbate the gap in access to resources for low-income or disadvantaged groups when entry rules to either supply or demand are altered. Thus, constraints on resource mobility, especially labor, may be worsened by relief efforts that do not account for the resource needs of these groups.

CONCLUSION

Our understanding and experience with actually creating markets where previously they were highly restricted or missing is limited to a handful of cases. Even using the assumptions of the Business as Usual scenario, however, we learn that making markets is often a difficult and challenging task. In part, this may result from the political objective to make highly competitive markets in conditions that, at best, support only very noncompetitive exchange structures. Thus, where risk or temporal dimensions are critical to the perceived gains from trade, market structures are likely to be slow to replace the structures that rely heavily on less flexible rules for allocations.

From the discussion of relief efforts, it appears that intimate structures are very self-sufficient, with one great flaw: They rely largely on the external system for many of their needed goods. In the local relief area, the intimate and associational structures may initially play a very important role, but once reconstruction or development is underway, their roles are likely to be absorbed into the formal market structures where they become facilitative and integral to day-to-day operations. Continuity in the national institutions that currently support market activities makes this transition likely. Similarly, we expect property rights and the use of currency and credit in the relief area to be restored quickly to the levels of mechanisms and procedures used in the current U.S. economy.

Government restoration programs in the relief area are likely to be aimed at encouraging both perfectly and imperfectly competitive market structures. There may be an increase in the competitiveness in the region because of both the inflow of restoration funds and the government efforts to reduce transaction costs. According to the empirical studies of disaster areas, however, supply and demand improvements do not persist over time.

Outside the relief area, exchange activities are likely to be conducted with little reference to the relief activities. The fourteen functions previously described illustrate how interdependent these markets are with the myriad of formal institutions in the United States. In fact, without the support of the formal institutions, many of the existing markets would fail to operate or, at least, would be far less extensive than they are currently. Yet the institutions also provide market structures with a good deal of resiliency because they can isolate and address disruptive events to avoid widespread market failures.

6

The Wasteland: Worst Case

In complete contrast with Business as Usual, the *Wasteland* scenario is based on the assumption that vital resources are destroyed or degraded or, for a variety of reasons such as war or natural disaster, they are inaccessible or unusable. At the same time, the institutional framework of society is either historically underdeveloped or, for all practical purposes, completely eliminated.

The Wasteland may also apply to areas that had previously relied on resources and government direction from a central administration but have subsequently been cut off. Hence, the Wasteland is distinguished from the Bureaucratic Nightmare scenario where government and financial institutions exist in areas of low resources, as well as from the scenarios where resources are plentiful. The Wasteland, however, may exist in some parts of a country, or in some countries in the world, at the same time that the Bureaucratic Nightmare and Fat of the Land scenarios are operative elsewhere. It is presumed that the Wasteland areas are geographically or socioeconomically isolated from resource rich communities and are unable to obtain institutional or physical support from these other areas.

Of course, unless a society is rigidly divided both socially and spatially, such as South Africa under apartheid, the Wasteland scenario is unlikely to coexist with Business as Usual in the same society because development of some areas will substantially extend to all others, albeit unevenly. Similarly, in the worst cases brought about by destruction rather than underdevelopment, the central government would declare a state of emergency in a stricken zone and provide material and institutional aid to maintain civil order.

At this point, it may be worthwhile to remember that the Wasteland is defined as the extreme logical possibility. If sufficient institutional infrastructure exists at national, regional, or local levels to preserve the peace and security of civil society, then we have either the Business as Usual scenario or the Bureaucratic Nightmare scenario, depending on the level of resources. If the level of population is such that the resource base provides per capita plenty, we have the resource abundant condition of Fat of the Land and not the Wasteland.

LIFE WITHOUT CIVIL SOCIETY

The absence of institutions assumes no currency or banking system. With no records of debt and property ownership, possession is likely to be the principal determinant of ownership. In cases where such institutions had existed but were destroyed, preexisting contracts, therefore, would be likely to fall into abeyance. The absence of a law enforcement infrastructure to uphold even the rights of possession would exacerbate both the insecurity of property ownership and the risks of attempting to trade. This is especially true because trust in trading is already limited by the absence of institutions such as insurance and producer/consumer legislation. Monitoring, dispute settlement, and enforcement rests with individual traders or is the responsibility of individuals and groups with the physical power to coerce.

The existence or emergence of warlords, armed factions, dacoits, and bandit groups, is well documented in societies that have experienced a serious breakdown of the national institutions of civil society and in those societies where no such institutions have been established. Indeed, in the past, the existence of such groups (combined with a desire to quell class riots and internecine wars) was one of the reasons for the development of formal, state supported enforcement agencies and control institutions. Often, these state agencies of social control were recruited initially by the very armed factions that were the subject of control measures. Even in their early establishment, precise loyalty to the state was ambiguous. The case of Jonathan Wild, the first Thief-Taker General of Great Britain and Ireland (1715–1725), is instructive here. Wild was simultaneously responsible for the policing of London and the organization of a fencing operation employing thieves, whose loyalty to Wild would be ensured by his power to prosecute (Howson, 1970).

Paradoxically, in cases where established control institutions and central authority have been destroyed as in areas of natural disaster, this process is reversed. Disaster relief workers give many accounts of armed groups whose members are often the remnants of the very institutions that normally would be used to preserve order in emergencies and to maintain the conditions for the functioning of markets or orderly allocation of relief supplies. Units of law-enforcement agencies and military regiments have been observed (e.g., in Somalia, Uganda, and Kampuchea) to act as independent forces, collecting their own taxes on the movement of goods and appropriating services (Heder, 1980). Their strength relies partly on their possession of firearms but also on preexisting association and identification of common interests.

Similar phenomena have been encountered throughout the development of the United States, especially under the frontier conditions that parallel those of the Wasteland scenario in respect to the availability of resources and institutions of civil society. Take, for example, the activities of the notorious Judge Roy Bean of New Mexico (Sonnichsen, 1986), whose self-interested interpretations and enforcement of the law ensured his own enrichment. The California gold rush produced individuals such as John Sutter who, far from the reach of the state authorities, levied taxes on miners and working property to which he had no title (Umbeck, 1976).

It may be argued that Sutter and his ilk differed from those living under the conditions of the Wasteland scenario in that the frontiersmen were attempting to carve out a society in a land where no Europeans had previously established the rule of law. According to this view, economic development does not parallel economic breakdown. It may be thought that survivors of destruction attempt to reaffirm the rules by which they previously lived. The men and women who built the frontier society, however, came from places where the rule of law was well established. By no means were all of these characters misfits or fugitives who rejected the institutions of the civilized east. If all that were necessary for continuity in the effective rule of law between eastern city and the western frontier was that the values of civil society were carried in the heads of individual settlers, why could they not carry them effectively across space and time?

The answer is that effective and recognized values require an appropriate institutional framework. Eventually, such a framework diffused from east to west across the United States. In the meantime, the institutions, like kinship, that did move with the settlers, frequently substituted for the functions of civil society. At the family level, clan leaders like "Devil Anse" Hatfield and Judge James Hargis emerged as family enforcers around whom feuding groups, loosely tied by bonds of kinship and marriage, rallied for protection (Harris, 1940; Jones, 1948).

From the perspective of life in Western capitalism approaching the twenty-first century, some may find the Wasteland case unthinkable and therefore unrealistic. But, no matter how unpalatable, the Wasteland is conceivably thinkable and, therefore, it provides a logical bounding condition for economic recovery or for economic development. In this extreme scenario, more than any other, the absence of institutional continuity and patterns of social organization combine with extreme competition for resources to shape the bases for behavioral expectations. In accordance with our argument about the conditions affecting core values, these circumstances render any practical reliance on existent values and expectations of consistent human behavior highly unlikely.

If, by definition, the institutions of civil society are absent, we must ask what exists instead. In the long term, people are able to develop appropriate institutions of civil society given certain conditions. In so doing, they lift their communities out of the Wasteland scenario. In the short term, whether because of underdevelopment or destruction, they have to contend with some different options. One such pattern, particularly prevalent in some Third World countries such as Colombia and Peru, is that control and enforcement emanates not from the national government but from armed bandits living deep in the jungle who are organizing and controlling the production and distribution of narcotics. Similarly, in situations of First World devastation, survivalist groups in rural areas and territorial urban street gangs may be well adapted to step into any power vacuum left by the elimination of effective formal institutions that defines the Wasteland. Thus, it is reasonable to argue that the Wasteland scenario, regardless of its real world cause, provides conditions in which the criminal variant of the associational exchange structure may flourish.

As Hobsbawm (1969) points out, however, not all banditry is motivated purely by personal gain. The phenomenon of social banditry, where goods are expropriated from unwilling owners for distribution among the wider population, has been found in diverse times and places from the medieval Robin Hood to the James Gang of the U.S. frontier. Jesse and Frank James gained a strong following in mid-America following the Civil War for their activities against the unpopular banks and railroads (Settle, 1966). More recently, neither the Mafia nor the Carabinieri paramilitary police were equal to the challenge of Salvatore Giuliano, who exerted control over rural areas of Sicily in the years immediately following World War II (Hobsbawm, 1969). The situation surrounding Peruvian coca production has a similar pattern in that the local rural population provide social, material, and moral support to the armed groups who are providing local growers protection and oppose attempts by both their own government and U.S. interdiction agents to control drug crops through the use of defoliants.

In these circumstances, gang leadership is a major outlet for entrepreneurship of a certain sort. Other kinds of enterprise can be opened up by the removal of predisaster institutions and interregional markets, alongside a wholly changed demand and supply environment. The profit opportunities would have to be extremely large relative to investment, however, to compensate for both the economic risk of coordinating resources and the personal risk of having them expropriated by coercive threats or force (Knight, 1921). Indeed, a likely cost to an individual or community attempting to meet agricultural or manufacturing demands will be that of security, whether by hiring mercenaries or by organizing, training, and maintaining an armed militia. Citizens wishing to protect themselves from predatory gangs and unwilling to accept the patronage of social bandits may well choose the collective self-help option of organizing their own defense. The problems of an egalitarian, cooperative organization, however, have been well documented (Olson, 1965; Henry, 1985; Rayner, 1988). This option is likely to be facilitated by the charismatic leadership of individuals possessing the gifts of inspirational rhetoric and organizing skills to establish effective vigilante groups.

The vigilante solution to the problem of maintaining civil order where the formal legal institutions are weak has been a ubiquitous feature of U.S. history. The first recorded indigenous U.S. vigilante movement occurred in South Carolina in 1767 as a response to the problem of maintaining law and order far from the centers of effective government jurisdiction. It was a pattern repeated time and again beyond the Appalachians, culminating in vigilantism's most famous failure, the Wyoming cattlemen's regulator movements that precipitated the Johnson County War of 1892 (Brown, 1979).

An alternative source of dispute settlement may develop around charismatic holy men, corresponding to the Swat Pathan saints described by Barth (1959). Leaders of rival groupings may recognize that the transaction costs of settlement through violent confrontation are bound to be high. If the followers of A and B kill each other in a feud, both parties may be weakened in respect to a third contender. Powerful leaders may, therefore, prefer to submit disputes to some form of arbitration by a normatively disinterested third party who derives authority from sacred, rather than secular power. Another source of arbitrating authority may come from the possession of technical skills that confer power over natural resources rather than from a coercive power over individuals or groups. In either case, physicians and priests, for example, may well prove capable of maintaining a market peace free from intervention by rival parties who rely on the arbitrational powers of these individuals. Developments in Eastern Europe have also confirmed that, as in the post-Communist state of Hungary, respected artists, playwrights, and authors may be the only figures that command respect and trust of the postrevolutionary populace.

Arbitrators are not the sole alternatives to violent confrontation.

Large-scale exchanges of prestige goods and competitive feasting are examples of "Fighting With Property" (Codere, 1950) that have supplanted warfare in places as diverse as the American Northwest Coast and Papua New Guinea (Strathern, 1971). This activity is paralleled in nineteenth- and twentieth-century America by the competitive philanthropy of robber barons and multimillionaires, who enhanced the power and influence of their families by establishing foundations and endowing the hundreds of university chairs that bear their names. Hence, the prestige exchange structure is likely to be highly significant in establishing a status hierarchy for dispute settlement between individuals competing for leadership roles either in gangs or in self-protective communities.

The bandit, brigand, or dacoit gang may be an important unit of consumption (by appropriation) and of exchange, through both prestige and criminal markets. It also may be a provider of military or security services and a regulator of economic activity through taxation and provision of a market peace. Thus, peasant marketplaces may emerge under the patronage of an enforcer (as well as an arbitrator) who is capable of maintaining civil order and arbitrating smaller disputes among traders. In all of these cases, however, the principal unit of production is the extended family (including people treated like kin), which will account for the exchange and consumption of subsistence goods through intimate and associational exchange networks.

Hence, it certainly is not the case that all exchange under the Wasteland scenario is subject to coercion. Neither are all contracts enforced through threats of violence. The true free market does not seem to be an important option here, however, because most exchanges are conducted according to socially defined webs of obligation that hold together the self-protective community just as surely as they bind the charismatic leader to his followers.

The risk reducing benefits of intimate and associational trading relationships are especially appreciated in a climate of high uncertainty (Mintz, 1961). Such relationships are likely, therefore, to encourage preferential trading partners in the peasant marketplace, which seems to be the closest to the free market that society can hope to aspire while the Wasteland conditions apply. Until the situation improves such that the Wasteland bounding conditions are alleviated, preferential trading relationships seem likely to be maintained, despite the danger that this may result in a decline in the quality of goods traded (Wilson, 1980).

In summary, subsistence, prestige, and peasant market exchange structures, all heavily influenced by intimate and criminal associational exchange, are likely to anticipate or displace many formal market activities under the conditions of the Wasteland.

HIGH RISK AND SCARCITY

Except in those increasingly rare cases where indigenous sustainable systems remain relatively immune from the pressures of the wider economy, subsistence production under the Wasteland is not likely to be "the original affluent society" that Sahlins (1972) ascribes to the Kalahari Bushman. It may be that Bushmen have adopted a "zen road to affluence" by restricting wants to those limited range of resources that are plentiful in the desert for those with appropriate skills. We may be able to emulate a Bushman restraint on wants under the Fat of the Land scenario where certain goods are plentiful; however, despite superficial similarities that arise from the narrow variety of resources available to both Bushmen and, for example, the landless rural poor, other factors render the comparison tenuous.

For the Bushman, restriction of wants depends on living where other groups do not put competing pressures on resources. True, where others see only desolation in the desert, the Bushman may see wild orchards and abundant game (Lee, 1969). This was not always so, however. Bushmen have learned their ability to extract plenty from scarcity because stronger groups forced them out of places where nature's bounty is more obvious. Bushman affluence depends on acquired skills and controlling population. It also depends on their former persecutors not following them into the desert to compete for its simple fruits.

The Wasteland scenario is not one in which human societies have adapted to resource scarcity without extensive institutional infrastructure beyond the kinship unit. It is one in which populations are deprived of resources and institutions either by moving or being moved to rural frontier areas or marginal urban shanties or because their endowments are removed by war or natural disaster.

The Wasteland places everyone in the desert in competition for what resources exist or remain and with little guarantee of an adequate transition period for social learning to acquire new skills to extract plenty from scarcity and to learn to view the world of goods in a new way. Rather, the Wasteland is likely to be an undignified scramble for resources to sustain life in the short term. This will be accompanied by the formation and dissolution of shifting alliances between individuals and groups, as community stalwarts, politicians, religious leaders, entrepreneurs, criminals, police, and military units vie with each other to establish control over local populations.

The highest priorities of people living in the Wasteland is likely to be finding shelter, food, water, medications, tools, and weapons. Secondary demand will be for items that may be useful for future barter or for modification to other uses.

The quantity of resources thus assimilated, however, probably will be

limited to those that can be carried by persons, on animals, or in hand-
carts. Where motor vehicles are available, gasoline supplies (according
to our definition of resource availability) are likely to be extremely limited. The necessity to defend acquisitions from seizure by others constitutes a limitation on stockpiling by individuals, groups, or
communities. Hence, there is a motivation for ordinary citizens to organize vigilante groups, to seek membership in gangs, or to seek the
protection of enforcers.

Competition for durable goods is likely to be limited by their finite
supply. Those that are durable may enter the prestige sphere and be
used in dispute settlement or to pave the way for the trade of nonprestige
goods between rival groups (Malinowski, 1922; Singh Uberoi, 1962).
Subsequently nonprestige goods will be produced in the domestic mode
with a strong emphasis on subsistence exchange. The domestic mode
of production, combined with the vulnerability of civil society, is likely
to yield six major problems for exchange within this scenario.

- The absence of currency and the scarcity of resources will result in low
  purchasing power. Scarcity of agricultural and domestic productive capacity
  means that supply is fixed. Relative prices for food will escalate dramatically.
  Prices would be only a means of communicating comparative value; no
  money would actually change hands because barter, or currency substitutes
  such as precious metals, or even cigarettes, may completely displace cash
  transactions. Items and quantities exchanged are likely to replace cash equivalencies as indicators of value.

- Resources that do exist are consumed in the short term. As conditions stabilize, rising demand may continue as traditional technologies are developed
  to replace lost raw materials or productive capabilities and new skills are
  developed. Credit, within a barter economy, is likely to prove problematic
  given the high uncertainty of the environment. Where long-term trading
  relations are established between preferred trading partners and where prestige exchanges develop between leaders or communities, credit will be available, but it is unlikely that there will be an open market or general use of
  credit among traders.

- Given the absence of vital resources, there will be binding time constraints
  on all production and exchange activities in order that the population can
  assure its own survival.

- There will be an abrupt shifting of demand and supply as supplies are
  damaged and preferences altered by the deterioration of resources and loss
  of institutional structure. Market power balances may be shifted decisively,
  as goods once valued and representative of wealth are reevaluated. Their
  owners may be instantly poor while others, particularly those with coercive
  power or skills essential to survival, become wealthy and powerful.

- The loss or movement of the population or the unavailability of records of
  property ownership and absence of the institutions to enforce contracts, also

may lead to dramatic changes in the distribution of wealth as debtors are freed of their obligations at the expense of creditors.

- The resultant free-for-all is very likely to produce considerable conflict based on perceived injustices and the scramble for control of surviving resources.

FUNCTIONS

Under the Wasteland scenario, the subsistence, peasant marketplace, criminal variant of the associational and prestige exchange structures may fulfill the necessary and facilitating functions of a market. In describing the mechanisms that accomplish those functions, it is appropriate to consider the institutions available or those that can be created to operate the mechanisms. Clearly, under the Wasteland scenario, the ability to perform functions will depend on (1) the transferability of functions from inoperative institutions; (2) the perceived legitimacy of the functions and of any institutions established for carrying them out; and, (3) the time taken to adapt mechanisms and develop alternative institutions for the performance of the necessary functions. These are dealt with in the following section.

Define Property Rights

The scarcity of resources and the absence of an infrastructure render it questionable that traditional or predisaster patterns of land tenure will survive. Possession of land and the power to protect it may prove to be the criteria of ownership for agricultural production. Subsistence production/consumption units probably will be able to farm as much land as they have labor power within the family unit, as extended to include close friends and their kin.

The subsistence structure is so closely dependent on membership of a multipurpose social group that rules governing shared property rights actually constitute major social bonds. Internally, therefore, there is no need for an extra-market legal system and rights are defined and enforced internally by kinsmen and coresidents. Externally, property rights probably will be enforced by vigilante groups or gangs, although neutral mediators (such as religious leaders, doctors, or artists) also may participate in their definition. Personal private property is likely to be very limited in scope.

Similarly, property rights in the prestige structure depend strongly on custom and kinship. Violators of rules defining these rights are excluded from transactions by other members of the market. However, in some cases, extra-market sanctions may be brought to bear by enforcers to decide disputes over property by force of arms.

Property rights in the peasant marketplace structure probably will be defined through the development of customary rules interpreted by community or gang leaders, who allocate disputed resources, and market patrons (sometimes the enforcers, but also religious figures, guilds, etc.) who maintain the market peace. These are extra-market mechanisms.

Convey Supply/Demand Information

The subsistence and peasant marketplace structures effectively convey information. The subsistence structure does this through intimate face-to-face interaction, while the peasant marketplace structure brings traders to a common marketplace, precisely to reduce information costs. The prestige exchange structure provides motives to restrict information because the object is to bring about status enhancing exchanges, usually at the expense of rivals (Codere, 1950; Strathern, 1971).

Provide Opportunity for Legitimate Transactions

A variety of institutional mechanisms, primarily kin and friendship based trading networks, provide opportunities for legitimate transactions. Also, certain sites such as churches or their remains might provide safe locations for trade with members of other such networks, especially if presided over by community leaders or holy men, to keep the market peace. The purpose of peasant marketplaces is to provide transaction opportunities, reduce information costs, and mitigate risk.

Mechanisms such as blood brotherhood (Barth, 1959) or patronage (Eisenstadt and Roniger, 1984) provide security for itinerant traders or for those venturing into territory beyond the immediate community.

Exchanges internal to the production/consumption group are likely to be legitimated through rules that specify continuing social relations. Mealtimes may be the most formal occasion of exchange here. Just as in all exotic and industrial societies, religious festivals, rights of passage, weddings, and anniversaries frequently are occasions for prestige prestations (Douglas and Isherwood, 1978).

Limit Provisions of Legitimate Contracts

In the subsistence structure, this is done by the rules of distribution within the production/consumption group. Peasant marketplace structures combine traditional trading patterns with the extra-market controls of landowners and market patrons. The rules of prestige exchange limit legitimacy in that system.

Within these broad limitations, the provisions of legitimate contracts are largely a matter of individual negotiation between traders, although customary rules of conduct and demands made by kin and friendship networks, churches, and community associations constrain the terms of contracts made within the group. Contracts with outsiders or members of other communities probably will be less constrained, except in the burdens placed on the whole network by the undertakings of a single member. If an individual defaults on an obligation, his or her entire production/consumption unit will be called on to make redress by the injured party's community group or powerful patron (Gluckman, 1955a and 1955b).

Enforce Contracts Other than by Physical Coercion

Ultimately, the threat of coercion by the possessors of military force seldom will be far from the minds of major disputants. All of the exchange structures imply some sort of enforcement of contracts, however. The nature of enforcement varies from social pressure and shaming in subsistence and prestige structures to a combination of the desire for repeat transactions and extra-market constraints from market patrons in peasant marketplaces.

Settle Disputes

There is only a very limited range of sanctions and appeals available in the Wasteland scenario. In subsistence and prestige structures, threats of exclusion (as well as shaming and ostracism) encourage settlements. In peasant and criminal associational structures, these mechanisms are supplemented by extra-market agencies. As stated above, the neutrality of holy men and artists, and their separation from the daily power struggle, may be respected by parties to a dispute. Leaders may employ oracular mechanisms to make decisions without their attribution to human agency (Evans-Pritchard, 1937). Another mechanism is contests, including fighting, tests of physical endurance, or the giving away of a valued endowment in the prestige structure. Talking directed at settlement (Roberts, 1979), on the other hand, might include third-party adjudication imposed by a judge or arbitrator, mediation by a go-between or holy man, and consensus formation through extensive debate (Rayner, 1988).

Maintain Civil Order

The subsistence structure depends on the intimate relations of the production/consumption group to maintain civil order, and this is also a strong factor in the prestige and peasant structures. Because of the weaker social bonds between exchanging partners in the peasant system, it additionally relies on extra-market agencies, such as military leaders or priestly market patrons, to maintain market peace. Ultimately, civil order will depend on those who have the guns, whether they are community vigilantes, entrepreneurial mercenaries, or former police and military units.

Legitimate Other Functions

Subsistence structures legitimate all internal functions through their multipurpose social relations. Social relations based on coresidence, kinship, or established trading relationships are also important in prestige and peasant marketplace structures, but they are supplemented by the extra-market control system. In the criminal associational exchange structures, legitimation relies on the interplay of threatened coercion and promised protection from outsiders to the group.

Guarantee Currency and Close Substitutes

There are no currencies in subsistence exchange. In the prestige exchange structure, the prohibition on exchanging down prestige goods for subsistence goods guarantees their value as close currency substitutes (Bohannon, 1959; Douglas, 1967). In general, peasant markets use currencies that are either guaranteed by market forces (e.g., precious metals or predisaster divisible valuables like certain brands of cigarettes, as in the case of Kents in Romania) or else are externally guaranteed by extra-market forces, such as the state. By definition, the backers of fiat currencies are absent in this scenario. Guaranteeing emerging currencies or substitutes, therefore, will depend to some extent on the existence of those with appropriate assay skills. Experience in Kampuchea and Uganda indicates a strong likelihood that gold and gemstones will emerge as currencies when paper money fails (Heder, 1980). Some guarantor of authenticity will be required.

Administer Distributive Justice

Subsistence exchange structures administer distributive justice through rules of sharing. Prestige exchange structures rely on the needs of the status seeker to coordinate accumulation of goods to exchange. Regressive distribution of resources will occur where communities are at the mercy of enforcers who levy taxes in exchange for protection.

Monitor and Modify Operations in Response to Changing Circumstances

This function is performed by all of the exchange structures in the Wasteland. There is likely to be a tendency for fixed allocation rules in both the subsistence and prestige structures to change the slowest once they have become established; however, the low level of resources suggests that many rules will have to be flexible or the groups will perish.

Mitigate Risk

This will depend primarily on information and risk spreading activities on the part of traders. In all four exchange structures, established trading relationships mitigate risk. Although not a requirement in peasant marketplace structures, small traders frequently display a preference for developing a limited number of steady customers to whom they give a small advantage (Mintz, 1961). They avoid selling to only one customer, however, in order to disperse risk (Scott, 1976). *Ex ante* payments also reduce risk in peasant markets. Peasant producers reduce risk by use of multiple seed varieties, farming on scattered strips, and so forth. Formation of multiple trading units, consisting of multiple households or communities, can distribute losses, but they also will require a disbursement of gains from trade. Preference for a series of small transactions over a few large ones may increase transaction costs, but they will reduce the size of potential losses through default of payments, fraud, or short-term price fluctuations.

Exploit Comparative Advantage, Specialization, and Division of Labor

These economic enhancements do not exist in subsistence exchange structures. In prestige and peasant structures there is a clear tendency to exploit such differences where possible, but traditional patterns of work and low levels of technology constrain this possibility. Where it occurs, exploitation of specialization is likely to depend on what skills are available. Those who are in a position to enforce civil order or provide medical care, for example, may be able to extract a premium in transactions, even when they do not directly involve the use of those special skills. This is a form of credit used to create long-term obligations that make goods or services more widely available.

Reduce Transaction Costs for Intertemporal or Interregional Transactions

Fixed allocation rules reduce transaction costs in subsistence exchange structures. Where the imperative is to feed every group member and

maintain group cohesion, haggling over who gets what is counterpro-
ductive. Peasant marketplaces reduce transaction costs by seeking to
reduce information costs. Prestige exchange structures reduce information costs by public display associated with wealth transfers. Transaction costs associated with interregional trade, however, will be largely
a function of those maintaining civil order. Where civil order is not
maintained, transaction costs arising from risk will be high whether from
employing guards or from absorbing the costs of lost shipments. Payment of protection money or tariffs to enforcers will be one way to
mitigate risks of attack or theft. Such taxes themselves become transaction costs, however. To the same end, blood-brotherhood institutions
could be instituted between itinerant and resident traders.

CONCLUSION

We conclude by considering the interaction between functions and
sustainable exchange structures. The definition and maintenance of
property rights under the Wasteland scenario are extremely problematic.
Whilst participation in subsistence production and consumption may be
predicated on kinship and close friendship, the ultimate enforcers of the
collective property rights of the subsistence group are those who command the resources of the prestige sphere and those who control the
peasant marketplace by virtue of military strength.

Barter, rather than currency, may be favored for everyday exchanges
of subsistence goods. Within the production/consumption group, systems of fixed allocations, perhaps initially based on the perceived special
needs of children or on bonds of affection to the elderly, will establish
equivalent values. In the peasant marketplace exchanges, negotiation
according to supply availability, transaction costs, and demand will establish values. Currency is likely to be confined to the prestige sphere
or to be used for obtaining particularly lumpy goods.

Major shifts in demand and supply are likely to result from the prevalence of the Wasteland conditions. There will be a strong incentive for
communities voluntarily to restrict the range of wants among members
in order to avoid the disruption of demands that cannot be satisfied. In
chapter 3 we referred to the social methods of income leveling and
restraints on conspicuous consumption among West Yorkshire coal miners in order to maintain the cohesion of the community. The pressures
on subsistence groups to eschew activity that might divide one section
of the group against another are likely to be even stronger in the Wasteland than in contemporary England.

Enforcers or other leaders will coordinate prestige activity. These leaders are able to provide nondivisive incentives (a share in his prestige)
for subsistence groups to cooperate in the provision of public goods.

For example, Pospisil (1963) describes how only the prestigious big man could persuade his fellow Papuans to collaborate in the construction of a bridge and how each villager retrieved his own logs from the structure when it fell into disrepair after the big man's influence had waned. The coordination of labor for large collective projects is likely to be a major obstacle to economic development in the Wasteland, especially where middlemen are dependent on enforcers for protection at the same time as their opportunities are limited by the prevalence of fixed allocations of goods.

7

Fat of the Land: Resource Abundance

The scenario of resource abundance, or the *Fat of the Land* scenario, is based on the assumption that endowments, consisting of both material resources, such as machinery and goods, and nonmaterial resources, such as skills and knowledge, are available and relatively plentiful. In contrast to the Business as Usual scenario, however, the overall system of social and political institutions whose functions facilitate existing demand/supply transactions is destroyed or underdeveloped. Thus, the institutions that interacted with market structures in Business as Usual are largely absent except at the local level.

Despite the absence of national and regional institutional infrastructures, we assume that a high level of available resources will be associated with local institutions including town and village councils, church congregations, voluntary organizations, and the kinship structure. Property rights will be recognized only if the owner is a member of the community. Property rights may be reallocated where owners live far beyond the reach of available communications abilities or because they are large corporations that were part of a national institutional structure that has collapsed. This process of the breaking up of state monopolies through privatization has occurred following the demise of the Communist infrastructure of Eastern Europe. Where nonowners already occupy property as renters or managers, possession is quite likely to become the criterion for the establishment of property rights, even if the fiction is created of holding the resource in trust for the original owner. Where there is no occupier or manager capable of managing the resource, allocations may include the creation of common property to be used under the control and on behalf of the community as a whole. Alternatively, it may be an open-access resource available to all comers to exploit as they wish, thus succumbing to the so-called tragedy of the commons (Hardin, 1968).

COORDINATION OF RESOURCES

The Fat of the Land scenario seems most likely to apply to rural areas. For this reason, most of our description will concentrate on rural examples. We do not, however, preclude the viability of urban rural areas under these conditions in which, for example, the direction of commuting is reversed as city dwellers sell their labor on farms. Other possibilities include small urban manufacturing enterprises that are able to adapt to the production of goods from local materials.

Where the distribution of resources is very skewed, the owners of land and agricultural resources and the owners of raw materials for emerging craft skills may take on the role of organizing productive labor. Those who do not control agricultural land and seed stocks will not be able to produce the diversity and quantity of foodstuffs necessary to support their families. Single families may not have access to sufficiently large plots of land to be fully self-supporting. Many will have merely their labor power to trade. Landowners may be unable to use mechanized agricultural equipment, partly because of the lack of gasoline and partly because they are likely to diversify their crops because of the absence of centralized national markets.

Where resources are evenly distributed throughout the community, for example, in an area consisting almost exclusively of small family farms, the absence of formal government infrastructure is likely to generate coordination problems for a community of equals in the areas of communications, transportation, marketing, and the provision of public goods.

Whatever the distribution of resources, two major forces will influence the recovery or development of resource coordination for exchange and production in the Fat of the Land scenario. First, with the absence of monitoring, dispute resolution, and enforcement infrastructure, there will be only loose constraints governing market opportunism (Williamson, 1985). In effect, traders may be likely to violate implicit or explicit exchange agreements where sanctions and enforcement are weak. This would increase the uncertainty of trade, making exchanges with temporal, spatial, or principal-agent obligations much more costly to trading agents.

Second, the absence of developed infrastructure and interregional market structures, in combination with the demand/supply environment, would shape a particular set of opportunities for trade. As Kirzner (1973) points out, it is the existence of unexploited opportunities for earning profits that stimulates middleman behavior. This view is consistent with Schumpeter (1964), where firms are motivated by potential profits to create new ways of doing things and new things to do. Where resources are plentiful but institutional infrastructure is lacking, many ways of doing things will be severely restricted or undeveloped. However, the availability of resources will be an incentive for some people to innovate. Evidence from self-help businesses suggest that innovations are more likely to develop where preset guidelines are at a minimum (Knight and Hayes, 1982). The issue of opportunity as an incentive to trade needs some qualification, however, in light of the Eastern European experience. Here it has been shown that, in spite of new opportunities, a population used to central planning and bureaucratic decision making is reluctant to take risks and is slow to innovate.

Even where middlemen readily grasp the available opportunities, their gains are likely to be limited by opportunism. Thus, profit opportunities will have to be large relative to investment to compensate these agents for accepting the risk of coordinating resources. In fact, the presence of extreme opportunism and the need to coordinate resources probably will discourage most loosely organized middlemen and lead to the emergence of organized corporate groups led by entrepreneurial managers. Knight (1921), in discussing the relationship between profit levels, resource coordination, and managerial control, argues that control of and responsibility for resource coordination is strongly identified with entrepreneurship and profit seeking.

Of special concern is how the opportunities for entrepreneurship will be taken, given the increase in uncertainty from opportunism. Williamson (1985) argues that a competitive market structure may sufficiently govern exchanges, where the goods are nonspecialized for the traders (middleman behavior). If impersonal exchanges are not possible then extra-market governing institutions, such as firms, contracts, and courts, will be necessary for stable exchanges.

It is important to recognize that the entrepreneurial role is not exclusively economic and is likely to fall on charismatic persons of high prestige such as clerics, respected community leaders and those emergent leaders who show particular skills for organizing. Thus, this part of the Fat of the Land system is strongly dependent on prestige exchange among organizers. Such organizers are likely to be recognized because of their roles in the associational exchange structures where they have proved their ability as wheeler-dealers. Thus, community organizers will correspond to the big men who mobilize individuals for major cooperative efforts to provide public goods as in traditional Papua New Guinea (Pospisil, 1963).

Participants in this scenario may cooperate to form production enterprises, especially in the urban organization of crafts and small manufacturing. As Durkheim (1893) points out, however, labor specialization makes members of a social unit highly interdependent, hence more vulnerable to risk. Paradoxically, the interdependence is between groups who perform specialized functions rather than among the members of such groups whose similarity to each other in terms of skill and social position is the basis of their social bonding.

The absence of external markets and their governing institutions is likely to result in a limited range of goods and services, even though resources may be abundant. Hence, we assume that the Fat of the Land scenario will revolve around a primary production/consumption unit based on the nuclear family. These units constitute a basic subsistence exchange structure. Where the primary family groups combine to form new social networks and extended families to share and pool resources, then the elements of intimate exchange structures occur. The reasons for a more familiar and intimate exchange structure are essentially the trading risks and the absence of trust among trading partners. Only those who are intimates or who are part of an established trading network are likely to be seen as trusted trading partners in the absence of an effective infrastructure that can guarantee exchange contracts. This may make it very difficult for middlemen to establish true market activity.

There will be entrepreneurial opportunities, however, particularly because, as we have said, resource abundance need not be an exclusively agricultural scenario. Where institutions have collapsed, through war, revolution, or economic withdrawal, hydroelectric or mine-mouth fossil plants, which are located in rural areas, may become a new focus of activity. With no responsibility to government or stockholders, local managers/operators may see themselves or their communities as owners of the plant and become either powerful monopolists or managers of these resources as common property. Similarly, any property, such as plant, machinery, and products located in rural or semirural areas, previously owned by a defunct government or national and multinational corporations, also may be claimed by local managers and, together with utility managers and other entrepreneurs, form the hub of an eventual rebirth of industrial production.

The absence of currency may be an initial obstacle to development because systems of direct barter tend to be inefficient, but this need not be the case under certain circumstances (Dalton, 1982; Leijonhuhvud, 1973). For example, barter may support trade where the medium of trade is scarce or money prices fail to adjust quickly to an economic environment that is radically changing. Where direct swaps do generate intolerable transaction costs, however, precious metals and jewels may prove to be close substitutes for currency, provided appropriate assay skills are available within the community. Another possibility in cooperative communities is the development of time contracts in which goods and services are exchanged for promissory notes of labor time. This has the convenience of being infinitely divisible from months to minutes, and the contracts for time may be legitimated by the dispute-settlement system should they not be honored.

For example, in the Comox Valley of Vancouver (Hart, 1986), a barter system called the Local Exchange Trading System (LETS) allows members to operate without money. Members of LETS submit information about the goods and services they have to offer for a notional green dollar amount. A member who wants another's service but has no money contacts the other member who provides the service and, through the LETS office, credits the supplier's account and decreases the demander's account. The supplier may require the services of others in the network who, because of this exchange, are able to employ the services of the original demander. The unit of exchange, the green dollar, remains where it is generated, providing a continually available source of liquidity. The ultimate resource of the community, the members' productive time, is never limited by lack of money (Meeks-Lowry, 1987). There have been no problems with members defaulting on repayment. This is explained by the intimacy of the network and the trust that has developed between the traders and for the system. Also, inability to pay is not a problem because green dollars never leave the community and are always able to be reearned; the currency cannot collapse because it is based on the time and skills of the members. Other possibilities for generalized exchange outside of such an intimate network are adumbrated by Hart (1986), including buckskins (the origin of the term "buck" meaning "dollar").

SURPLUS RESOURCES

The overall exchange system under the Fat of the Land scenario is primarily a combination of prestige exchange, peasant marketplaces, intimate, and subsistence exchange structures. These circumstances create conditions for the development of a perpetual surplus for small- to medium-sized communities.

These conditions may shape people's perceptions of satisfaction from manufactured goods, producing a constraint on wants that Marshall (1961) calls "material plenty," with a low standard of living, or what Sahlins (1972) calls the "zen road to affluence." Like Sahlins' hunter-gatherers, the Amish communities of Pennsylvania restrict the wants of their members with respect to consumer goods in order both to maintain group solidarity and to guarantee availability of capital for essential resources (Hostetler, 1963). Thus, both the Bushmen and the Amish are able to shape the utility functions of their members even, in the latter case, when they are constantly exposed to the wide range of goods that entice members of neighboring communities.

We suggest, therefore, that under conditions of resource abundance, people may view their pattern of wants as completely and infinitely satiable. Under these circumstances, there may be very little incentive to engage in economic activity for direct financial gains. Indeed, as the literature on hunter-gatherers suggests, production is likely to be low relative to its possible capacity; labor power under employed; and technological means under used, as are natural resources. Under these circumstances, surpluses would become available to trade, but, since all units have satisfied their own subsistence wants with a similar range of goods, trade is unlikely to occur. The possibility emerges that such a society will not create the critical level of diversity in endowments or preferences that Alchian and Allen (1969) identify as necessary to support the desire to exchange for financial gain.

Exchange may arise from other motives, however. Under conditions of resource abundance, elements of prestige exchange structures are likely to be present. The anthropological literature suggests that prestige exchange reduces the risk of trading where no formal regulation exists (Malinowski, 1922). In other words, moral regulation is substituted for formal regulation. Owing to the absence of money and the high search and transaction costs, trading for financial gain is undeveloped. Thus, in the Fat of the Land scenario people will use goods as a medium to create social bonding just as they do in poor urban areas at present (Stack, 1974; Dow, 1977). Indeed, Bell (1981) points out that relations of interpersonal trust regulated by customary ethics formed the basis of civil society from which the modern market system emerged. The world of Adam Smith was one of thousands of small family firms, of visible merchants and customers, so that Smith could look to civil society, not government, as the arena in which competition would be regulated by custom and ethics rather than by contract and law.

If prestige exchange forms the basis of civil society, which is itself the foundation on which the market system is built, we want to understand how prestige exchange might develop under resource abundance. Initially, persons with access to a limited supply of manufactured products may accrue considerable prestige from the acquisition of these scarce resources. The source of prestige, however, may expand to include domestically produced items at the point when all subsistence needs are met by the production/consumption unit. The possibility of prestige exchange to enhance social bonds is opened by the ability to produce large surplus quantities for competition regarding the amount of the good produced. The overall importance of the prestige exchange structure as an index of status relative to trade for financial gain increases because differences in absolute wealth will vary very little in the surplus environment. This is one of seven changes discussed below, which characterize the economics of a surplus trading environment.

- A major feature of the Fat of the Land scenario is the absence of money as a medium of exchange. In these circumstances, prices are likely to be determined though barter with the items and quantities exchanged displacing monetary prices as an indicator of value.
- The demand for a narrow range of agricultural products from the survival areas is likely to be relatively low. The major consumers of these products may not be there and the means to transport the products may be undeveloped or otherwise eliminated.
- Given the perceived surplus of vital resources and the virtual absence of all resources unnecessary for survival, time constraints cease to be binding. Nothing is particularly urgent, because everything needed is available and that which is not available is not of use.
- Although there may be few limitations on time so that, theoretically, the market system will eventually respond in the short to medium term, time makes very little difference to the excesses of available products.
- The levels of demand and supply of goods combined with the nature of preferences at this level of development may have a major impact on the value of assets and the distribution of wealth. Some goods, which in other circumstances are valued and representative of wealth, may be worthless in this context.
- In addition, where disaster is the cause of this level of development, destruction of records and property ownership is likely to render some debtors free of their debts and some creditors without claims to wealth.
- Under the Business as Usual and Bureaucratic Nightmare scenarios the possibility is present for government intervention in the distribution of resources. Under Fat of the Land, however, centralized government, by definition, is nonexistent or ineffective.

These seven factors suggest that exchange for financial gain is considerably limited, but the developments already discussed would produce a change in the kind of exchange rather than its reduction. Exchange for financial gain may be absent or displaced by self-sufficiency and the perceived surplus of food. This situation also is likely to be encouraged by defensive cultural strategies. As Siegel (1979) shows, threatened groups seek to defend their cultural identity, even at the expense of other interactions. Pueblo Indians, Black Muslims, Amish, Hutterites, and Mormons have enforced detailed and rigorous codes for the regulation of their members' behavior. They have increased cultural integration and intensified communications within the group while minimizing communication with outsiders.

FUNCTIONS

The Fat of the Land scenario will require that some of the fourteen functions of exchange institutions will be performed by institutional arrangements different from those operating under Business as Usual.

Define Property Rights

Property rights are likely to be defined by possession. The absence of central government or of urban economic and commercial centers, however, will leave some property, including that previously owned by corporations, states, or federal authorities, open for redefinition. This may be privately appropriated or claimed by the local governing body.

Convey Supply/Demand Information

Whatever social networks exist in the rural infrastructure will convey supply and demand information, supplemented by friendship and kinship networks and individual traders. A major problem may arise, however, for transfer of information between communities. This will need to be overcome if those developing craft goods and agricultural products are to trade with those who begin to resume industrial production. Traveling merchants, acting as middlemen, may also serve to carry information between communities although, unless these persons are already known and accepted in more than one place, this form of information exchange may be severely limited.

Provide Opportunity for Legitimate Transactions

Wholesale and retail outlets provide opportunities for legitimate transactions particularly in stores, farmers' markets, and flea markets. In addition, the farm and sites visited by numbers of people, such as churches and meeting halls, lend themselves to this function and are likely to be supplemented by kin- and friendship-based trading networks.

Limit Provisions of Legitimate Contracts

The provision of legitimate contracts within a community is likely to depend on the type of local property rights system. Decision makers holding positions of power within the community probably will supplement existing law with rules to protect their private interests. The rules of kin and friendship networks will constrain traders. In addition, where traders and farm cooperatives exist, a collective constraint may limit the possibility of exchanges that benefit individuals at the expense of the cooperative.

Enforce Contracts Other than by Physical Coercion

The same institutions that limit the provision of legitimate contracts are likely to carry out the enforcement of contracts, other than by physical coercion.

Settle Disputes

Dispute settlement may operate on a combination of various rules. The rural dispute settlement mechanism of settlement-directed talking is likely to be of the mediation and go-between type. Here justice is administered by negotiation. Participants bargain not only over the substance of the dispute but also over the rules and procedures that apply. Some attempt may be made to treat like situations in a consistent manner, but this will be flexible and open to negotiation, depending on the circumstances. Courts may be established but, in practice, justice is likely to be administered according to community consensus involving relatively arbitrary application of formal rules and procedures. Appeals may well be arbitrary and relatively informal compared with the Business as Usual or Bureaucratic Nightmare scenarios. In addition to these forms, greater use may be made of the private justice institutions. The result is likely to be a coexisting diversity of procedures for settlement that are institution specific and may range from authoritarian, through representative, to collective forms (Henry, 1983). The sanctions applied in any one of this range of dispute-settlement systems also may be specific to the institution but will tend more towards shaming, ostracism, and expulsion than to imprisonment, treatment, or fines because the services available to administer correctional facilities would be absent and, given the weakness of the formal enforcement infrastructure (lacking the authority of the state), collecting fines could be difficult. Sanctions against outsiders who transgress community rules may be punitive and harsh. Internal sanctioning, however, may be progressive, corrective, and restitutive, aimed partly at rehabilitation and partly to repair the breach in society. Finally, some settlement by contest may be present. This may take the form of the competitive destruction of property in abundance or the giving away of property that is valued.

Maintain Civil Order

The vestiges of centrally established institutions, such as courts and police, are likely to attempt to maintain civil order in the wake of societal catastrophe. As various enterprises and organizations assume responsibility for policing their own members, however, private policing may be a more common feature (South, 1988). Private policing is also likely where no effective centrally sanctioned authority has ever developed. Some conflict is to be expected between the private police of different land, utility, or factory owners, especially in the absence of a federal system of control. Community policing may be organized and take the form of volunteers, neighborhood watches, and generally avocational forms (Shearing and Stenning, 1987).

Legitimate Other Functions

The legitimation of other functions, including enforcement, will depend on community norms and the predominant style of leadership. Where the community structure is dominated by the concentration of resources in the hands of a few property owners, legitimation will tend to be their prerogative based on the power of private property ownership and, as Renner (1949) points out, in its implied right to control people. In contrast, where resources are more evenly distributed, legitimation ultimately flows from the charisma of entrepreneurial leaders and the democracy of participation and negotiation.

Guarantee Currency and Close Substitutes

Using a barter system without money as a medium of exchange, this function is unlikely to be performed, except insofar as those who trade need to guarantee for themselves the quality of their purchases.

Administer Distributive Justice

Rudimentary local institutions and some version of local taxes and sales taxes are the most likely instruments of distributive justice. Where charismatic or entrepreneurial leaders emerge, the redistribution of resources is one of their sources of status. Under such a system, too, prestige rather than goods may be the valued resource to be redistributed. Some churches and community associations also may perform this function.

Monitor and Modify Operations in Response to Changing Circumstances

Monitoring is part of the entrepreneurial role, but networks of kinsmen also will engage in the continuous flexible assessment of an entrepreneur's work. As resource ownership is relatively concentrated, the system is likely to have limited flexibility as the responsibility for monitoring probably will be concentrated in a few hands. Because the information systems are likely to be under developed, there will be less opportunity to make rapid changes than under the Business as Usual scenario.

Mitigate Risk

Mitigation of risk depends on the extent to which social bonding provides structural support. Risk is reduced, in part, by adopting a barter system and by trading within a community and among members of a social network. In this case, risk is mitigated by eliminating exchange between traders who are unknown to each other. Such trade will only continue with the emergence of trading middlemen, who make contact with demanders and suppliers and earn a return for accepting the risk of coordinating the desires of these two groups. Within a community of equals, risk is reduced by relying on the credit allowed and particularly by the institution of reciprocity. Preference for a series of smaller transactions rather than a few large ones reduces the risk of loss. Where resource ownership is more concentrated, risk reduction depends primarily on the preparedness of the private owners of land and utilities to underwrite the remaining elements of the rural infrastructure and to support coalitions of traders who wish to do the same.

Exploit Comparative Advantage, Specialization, and the Division of Labor

The extent of this exploitation is likely to be limited. Individual specializations may emerge in certain craft areas.

Reduce Transaction Costs for Intertemporal or Interregional Transactions

Such reductions are not an immediate concern in the Fat of the Land scenario. These transactions are unlikely to occur until specialized craft production or industry develops. When alternative communications and transportation are developed, special trading relationships may occur,

tariffs may be imposed, and more formalized policing may be introduced
to reduce the risk of theft.

CONCLUSION

In the Fat of the Land scenario we argue that the property rights issue
is of central importance, especially because there is no centralized authority external to the community that can regulate and enforce ownership. Irrespective of the concentration of resource ownership,
additional demands will be placed on the surviving community's capacity for the resolution of disputes, if only to settle issues of the fair
reallocation of surviving property, especially where this is of unknown
or uncertain ownership.

The Fat of the Land scenario is clearly different from a money-based
system and relies on a barter-based system out of necessity rather than
choice. We argue, too, that there are likely to be major differences in
supply and demand, as goods (which under different circumstances may
have satisfied wants of demanders) become scarce or unusable.

The Fat of the Land scenario indicates that one of the principal reasons
for developing social cohesion is to develop institutions of trust to facilitate production and trading. Where resource ownership is concentrated, replacement institutions may tend toward the authoritarian.
Where resources are more evenly distributed, prestige and informal
social control mechanisms are likely to substitute for formal regulation.
Finally, the Fat of the Land scenario provides significant possibilities for
development to an industrial market system because conditions are encouraging for innovation and middleman behavior.

8

Bureaucratic Nightmare:
Institution Intensive

The *Bureaucratic Nightmare* scenario is based on the assumptions that endowments and resources are poorly developed or abruptly limited but institutional infrastructure exists largely intact. For example, a plausible setting would be the survival of an urban location in a global disaster, perhaps a state capital, that depends on outside suppliers for food and many manufactured goods as well as raw materials for local production. Alternatively, development in the Eastern European countries fits the conditions of this scenario well. The low level of developed resources is assumed to extend to many physical resources that support intercity/interregional communications and transportation so that migration from the Bureaucratic Nightmare setting is either very difficult or involves a high level of cost or uncertainty. Thus, the government is faced with the oversight of its existing population under conditions of severely limited resources and a viable institutional infrastructure that includes a banking system, a system for the recognition, protection and enforcement of property rights, a political system, and a legal system for the settlement of disputes.

Our analysis of the exchange structures likely to prevail under the Bureaucratic Nightmare scenario differs from prior work in two important respects. (In particular, see the 1987 survey by Hill.) First, although the adaptation and efficacy of institutions to the severe resource constraints is a relevant consideration for our analysis, our underlying assumption is that institutions are highly developed. Second, we make no attempt to argue about optimal responses of the extra-market institutions. Our intention is to delineate possible responses based on empirical and theoretical evidence and some understanding of the exchange problems faced under the Bureaucratic Nightmare. As we stated in chapter 1, the determination of appropriate policy actions is more closely linked with the criteria of applicability and stability than with the criterion of optimal resource use, although these criteria are related.

A review of some of the literature on World War I and World War II U.S. economic policy; European reconstruction; postdisaster economic recovery; and the attempt to develop market mechanisms in post-Communist Eastern Europe, particularly Poland and Hungary, and in the former Soviet Union; provides a basis for identifying policy problems for the operating institutions with special reference to market activities. We include limited review of the extensive literature on centrally planned economies. While representing many of the conditions of the Bureaucratic Nightmare, most of the literature on centrally planned economies focuses on the inefficiencies and problems of centralized systems and not the relations among different types of exchange organizations. The attempts by Eastern Europe and the former Soviet Union to move away from the centrally planned economic structure toward a market economy, however, are highly relevant to addressing the transition out of the Bureaucratic Nightmare scenario to market economic activity, particularly in those cases where the institutionally intensive environment continues for an extended time. At the time of this writing, limited evidence is available, and it is largely journalistic in nature, but we have drawn on it where relevant to inform our argument.

MANAGEMENT OF SCARCE RESOURCES

Much of the literature that we reviewed derives from a policy perspective on disaster management. Hence, it generally makes the assumption, implicitly or explicitly, that government institutions survive or are sufficiently developed to manage the limited resources. (Otherwise, for whom would the authors be making policy recommendations?) This assumption, however, is tempered by considerations of how government institutions function where there are extremely low levels of technical capabilities, wealth, and information. The economic recovery and development literatures suggest the following six problems.

- Given the operation of a credible currency system in the absence of currency reform, there will be excess purchasing power. Excess purchasing power can lead to rapidly escalating prices in uncontrolled markets. This problem results from the large cash and liquid asset balances that consumers may have relative to the number of goods and services that they can purchase following the destruction or curtailment of resources.

- There may be special demands on the scarce resources resulting from disaster or development events. For example, demands may arise as resources are required for special medical services such as famine relief, for adaptation of traditional technologies that depend on lost or depleted raw materials, for development of new skills, and for the need to invest in expensive physical resources, such as communication and information systems. Another consideration is the exacerbation of factors underlying market failure, such as uncertainty and externalities, so that even viable resource markets may fail to operate without government intervention. As an example, the credit market is likely to have difficulty functioning given the prevalence of uncertainty about the future.

- Given the severe restrictions on vital resources, there will be a number of binding time constraints within which actions must be taken or population survival cannot be assured.

- There may be abrupt shifting in demand and supply curves as market supplies and preferences are highly destabilized by disaster or development events. These changes may not only affect prices and quantities but market power balances as well.

- Shifting of demand and supply curves will likely affect the value placed on assets and subsequently, the distribution of wealth. Such changes hold the possibility for economic instability and large winners and losers in financial wealth from small resource changes.

- The disruption of market and distribution arrangements will also affect financial wealth. For example, disruptions may result from the inability of market agents to fulfill contract obligations for financial transactions, production, and consumption where they cannot obtain resources confidently.

MARKET FLEXIBILITY

As Olson (1963) points out, one of the most difficult problems to be faced with severe restrictions on resources is the loss of flexibility in the economic system. Flexibility arises from the many possibilities for substitution in the production and consumption processes for goods and services. Thus, as prices rise for particular inputs, producers or consumers can usually respond by making substitutions with relatively cheaper resources or goods. Major disruption or absences in resource supplies will limit many of the substitutions that are technically possible. Lack of information and communication resources will also impede the ability of producers to respond with technological change.

Given no limitations on time, flexibility can be introduced to the economic system. Olson's preference for the use of the market system to direct resources is largely based on the assumption of nonbinding time constraints. The time dimension has been emphasized by Winter (1963), however, who points out that an environment reflecting the Bureaucratic Nightmare conditions will involve a race between the development of productive capacity and the depletion of inventories for vital goods and services to sustain the population.

Considering the problems to be addressed and the limitations on time, government decision makers in Bureaucratic Nightmare will have to decide if market structures can provide viable solutions for resource allocations. While an overwhelming number of recommendations from the research on postdisaster economic recovery support reliance on market structures (Hill, 1987), there are some important aspects of the Bureaucratic Nightmare scenario that make other solutions more likely for critical goods and services.

First, because market allocations are driven by the decentralized decision making of large numbers of traders, they necessarily take time to respond to changing market conditions. Thus, prices may reach prohibitively high levels for a large proportion of the population and remain there until demanders and suppliers find alternatives. How long the high levels persist depends on the level of market power exercised by suppliers as well as the rate of production and technical change. In addition, if barter is discouraged, the price adjustments may be delayed further by restricting the local demand and supply information produced by barter (Leijonhuhvud, 1973). The adjustment process of conventional price mechanisms may not be acceptable or even feasible in the Bureaucratic Nightmare environment for the markets in food, shelter, and medical services where the race between productive capacity and sustaining the population is likely to be most extreme.

Second, the prevalence of uncertainty is another obstacle for the ability of traders within market structures to formulate new plans and to respond to price signals. Third, the high development of institutions within a limited location will imply that they have relatively more administrative capacity than marketing skills, and this may impede market development. Finally, regulation and government control are not immune to the forces of supply and demand.

With respect to the first three aspects, analyses of World War II policies can be insightful. Given the U.S. and British policies during and after the war, a number of studies have noted how effective these governments were in managing the use of resources that were abruptly in short supply (Olson, 1963; deChazeau et al., 1946; Homan and Malchup, 1945). Olson argues that the success of British food programs during the war was largely due to the government's ability to encourage substitutions in production and consumption both to increase nutritional output and conserve scarce shipping and storage resources. The government placed controls on consumption, shipping, and agricultural production and significantly altered economic activity. Rationing, regulations, subsidies, and price controls controlled food consumption. A combination of production goals, regulation, and price incentives decreased the production of livestock and increased the production of cereals and grains. In the United States, the government exerted control to direct resources to the production of war materials and later to redirect these resources to peacetime production. Of special concern for the U.S. case was the potential for inflation and depression in the postwar transition because there was a surplus of labor. The British and American cases never approached a level of control implied by the concept of "disaster socialism" discussed by Winter (1968) and others. (Disaster socialism would imply a command system for all major allocations, that is, complete specification of who gets what and how much they get.) Rather, control was exercised through a system of select intervention to manage resources where the unaided market process was assumed to be inadequate to meet the country's needs. Furthermore, much of the success of these programs is attributed to the willingness of the population to comply with the restrictions, suggesting they enjoyed a substantial level of public support (Olson, 1963). This point is important with respect to managing control over the unstable supply and demand conditions of the Bureaucratic Nightmare scenario and seems to be ignored in many of the studies of postdisaster economic recovery. Given that government decisions are not immune to the demands of the governed, to what extent would government control of particular markets or select intervention be a preferred solution?

THE ECONOMICS OF PUBLIC REGULATION

The literature on regulation suggests that political decisions, especially those regarding regulation, are strongly influenced by the attempts of one or more groups to extract an income transfer from other groups (Stigler, 1971). These payments are transfers because they exceed the minimum payment necessary to cover the incremental real costs of resources in the provision of the goods or services and involve a transfer of one group's surplus-in-exchange to another group. More generally, the demand for regulation will depend on the costs of organizing the groups that benefit from the regulations and the potential gains from obtaining the regulations (Peltzman, 1976).

The costs of regulation include not only the resource costs of compliance but also the loss of support from the harmed groups to the extent that they are organized and aware of the costs being imposed on them. Thus, disparities in the costs of organizing groups that are decentralized can influence the decisions regarding market intervention (Arrow, 1969; Benson and Faminow, 1986).

In addition to the possibility of increased demand for regulation, we have several reasons to expect an escalation of government control and intervention into some markets that were largely unregulated in the predisaster or early development environment. First, in the Bureaucratic Nightmare scenario, government institutions are highly accessible, and it may be within their traditional roles to respond to requests for disaster compensation or development services. Second, the costs of organizing may be reduced by a much narrower scope of concerns for potential demanders of government actions. Further, groups may have the time to devote to the efforts of organizing, even if these resources are at first preoccupied with emergency activities. Third, given differential resource availability, there is likely to be some demand to resolve large inequities in the resource distributions. Fourth, motivations to demand regulation for the gain of market power or the protection of income can be expected to operate in Bureaucratic Nightmare as it does in all societies. In fact, these motivations may be even more prevalent in the Bureaucratic Nightmare scenario than in Business as Usual because there is likely to be less competition among market agents and the gains from favorable regulation vary inversely with the level of competition (Tollison, 1982). Finally, it has been argued that because personnel in public institutions face incentives that are largely status orientated and not financial, public managers generally attempt to increase budgets or institutional power rather than constrain costs (Niskanen, 1979).

Even if the government rejects the use of intervention and prefers using the price mechanism to allocate goods and services, this may be undermined by behavior in the private sector. In a study of the West Coast Gas Famine of 1920, Olmstead and Rhode (1985) argue that private firms in the petroleum industry voluntarily rationed gasoline without government intervention. Traditional explanations such as the threat of intervention or attempting to discourage market entry do not explain the rationing programs followed by leading oil companies at the time. The authors find a more convincing explanation in the conflict of short-term versus long-term goals:

> According to SOCal's past chairman, R. G. Follis, oilmen also viewed the purely economic consequences of a large, market-clearing price increase as detrimental to their long-run interest. SOCal's leaders saw the company's prosperity as integrally tied to the economic development of the West, and they accepted considerable responsibility for promoting that development. Given this attitude, Follis thought it would have been unwise to shock the economy with enormous fluctuations in oil prices. To encourage western economic development and the rapid conversion to petroleum fuels, industry leaders thought it essential to assure agriculture and business a guaranteed supply of energy. (p. 1054)

In addition, Olmstead and Rhode (1985) suggest that the perceived causes of the shortage influenced the decision to ration. Instigated by a drought and an illegal railroad strike, the industry sought to preserve the appearance of being fair and patriotic by not exploiting the situation for short-term gain.

Other studies have identified fairness in the wake of events beyond the control of market agents as affecting market behavior. Plott (1986) discusses some experimental economics studies that suggest that an allocation of property rights based on chance will lead agents to share the gains from trade in a more egalitarian way than when the rights are allocated on the basis of skill. Garner (1986) argues that people's feelings of inequity significantly influences their productivity. Thus, "how society slices the economic 'pie' generally affects the size of the pie" (Garner, 1986: 262). Such explanations have been used also in the analysis of public acceptance of risky technologies (Rayner and Cantor, 1987). Finally, Arrow (1969) and Hirshleifer (1985) argue that establishing a sense of the greater good through common property rules or public intervention can entice individuals to act in the public interest.

On the basis of these arguments, we should expect that the institutional infrastructure will be called on often to use selective intervention as a response to severe limitations in resources. It is possible, however, that such intervention will not affect all markets; in particular those for nonessential goods and services may remain relatively unregulated. While it is difficult to specify all the goods and services that are labeled "critical" in such a world, food, water, shelter, medical services, transportation, and labor markets are likely candidates.

Although we regard extra-market intervention as supportive but outside the rules governing market structures, we introduce regulated market structures in this chapter to demonstrate their implications for market rules. Unfortunately, past experience suggests that extra-market institutions will not respond with appropriate controls in every targeted market, or they often ignore compounding problems such as excessive purchasing power and incentive incompatibilities. Criticisms of the failure of government to balance market controls with appropriate fiscal and monetary policy dominate the economic recovery and development literature (Hill, 1987). Implicit in these criticisms is the debate over piecemeal policies versus holistic public policies.

The lack of balance in public intervention is often at the heart of the negative outcomes following the intervention in resource constrained environments. For example, the use of price and wage controls in post–World War II Germany was not balanced with monetary reform to reduce excess purchasing power and fiscal reform to subsidize investment in desired production capacity (Hill, 1987). Similarly, although regulatory reform to stimulate production was effective during the use of wage and price controls in the United States during the 1970s, the program was undermined by the expansionary fiscal and monetary policies early in the period (Pohlman, 1975). Finally, even if well-intended, the uncoordinated or unbalanced efforts of extra-market institutions often create shortages or disincentives to supply that will be conducive to the formation of market structures outside the legitimate market system.

Under the conditions of this scenario, it is possible that the government could elect to enter the market directly as a quasi-public trading agent, such as a corporation similar to the Tennessee Valley Authority, which was created to promote regional development through resource management. While the successful use of state-owned enterprises is quite common outside the United States, for example, in Canada, France, and the United Kingdom, they have had limited success in correcting market failures in the contemporary United States. A major exception is the use of local municipalities to produce and distribute electricity. Successful use of this type of instrument to facilitate market activities often depends on two factors. First is the governing authority's ability to obtain the resources necessary to operate such an enterprise. Second is the belief that the public sector has some comparative advantage relative to a similar private undertaking. Often it is the second factor that is lacking as a rationale for the U.S. case.

ACTIVE GOVERNMENT INTERVENTION

The exchange of nonessential goods and services will be affected by other markets for critical goods but may be free of additional government control. Production may be affected if the suppliers use resources that are essential for critical needs, and continued production of the nonessential good may even be prohibited. Given the heightened demands on productive resources, any continued production of nonessential goods will probably be small-scale and localized. In the case of abrupt changes, trade may continue for a time under the prior market arrangements, for example in a particular store, but as more and more resources are directed to critical activities, transaction cost considerations may force a consolidation of nonessential market activity to a peasant market structure with general marketplaces similar to flea or antique markets. Exchange in such public places inhibits extreme use of monopoly or monopsonist power and reduces marketing or advertising costs and search and informational costs. Given the extreme limitations of these resources, there are strong incentives to reduce the costs of exchange for nonessential goods.

The markets for critical goods and services are the most susceptible to government intervention to alter the market process. This follows from their importance to population survival and the conditions present to fuel the demand for regulation and control in these activities. We consider three areas of intervention that will affect the rules of market structures: regulatory controls, fiscal policy, and monetary reform. The first, regulatory controls, can affect any number of specific market rules, including the transaction rules. Fiscal policy and monetary reform have a direct effect on demand and supply, but in general, only indirectly affect transaction rules through changes in the degree of competition or market power (i.e., shifts in market structures).

Regulatory Tools

Stone (1982: 10) defines regulation as "a state-imposed limitation on the discretion that may be exercised by individuals or organizations, which is supported by the threat of sanction." In the analysis of unregulated market structures, discretion is often limited by technical or network constraints but is unconstrained by government intervention with the exception of illicit activities. Rules in the associational and criminal markets reflect indirectly the enforcement of regulations on legitimate activities.

For the Bureaucratic Nightmare scenario, the objectives of selective intervention through regulation are likely to be redirecting and expanding productive capacity, conserving targeted resources, and population maintenance. Achieving many of the objectives of the Business as Usual regulatory system are prohibitively expensive in the resource limited environment. Given few resources for regulatory innovation, regulators may rely on tools that are either very familiar or easily enforced. Three types of regulatory tools that have traditionally been used to affect market outcomes are production standards, rationing or fixed-allocation systems, and wage and price controls.

Production standards include regulations that specify minimum or maximum limits on inputs, outputs, or processes used by the production technology. These standards may specify particular inputs and outputs, as well as quantities and qualities to be used by producers. By imposing production standards, regulators can restrict the set of possible technology choices available to suppliers. Alternatively, regulators may expand technology choices by removing production regulations previously imposed by the regulatory system. As an example, regulators removed certain restrictions on livestock grazing on previously set-aside acreage to increase supplies of meat during the U.S. wage and price control period of the 1970s (Jones, 1975). Restrictions affecting either maximum or minimum quality levels may be imposed on the processes to prepare vital food, as the British did during World War I and II (Olson, 1963).

Production standards can be used effectively where compliance costs are reasonable. In general, they will affect supply by placing institutional constraints on resource mobility. Further, if the regulations appear unpredictable, they may become one of the major uncertainties facing suppliers and thus affect transaction rules. In the presence of opposition to government regulations, monitoring costs and reporting by suppliers to assure compliance will place an additional demand on resources. This demand tends to vary directly with the number of suppliers to be monitored.

Berenbeim (1981) argues that one unintended effect of production regulation is its differential impact on small and big firms. In essence, there may be economies of scale with respect to meeting regulations, especially in the demonstration of compliance. Monitoring costs will be lower with a few large producers than in an industry made up of many small suppliers. Less competitive, large firms can be more resilient to the impacts of increased regulatory costs because they tend to start from a position of excess profit margins in comparison to small, competitive firms. Thus, increased government intervention, undertaken to direct the flow of essential resources in short supply, may also be a contributing factor in increasing the concentration of market power. If regulatory costs are high, then the government may be forced to limit the numbers of legitimate suppliers by dictating or encouraging oligopoly or monopoly market structures in order to have a market at all.

Especially in World War I and II, rationing was commonly applied in situations where important resources were severely restricted. In addition, it was an important policy tool in the reconstruction plans of many European countries (Milward, 1984). There are several general ways a government may ration resources or goods. Allocation priorities can be imposed and thus alter the rules about who, when, or where the good may be demanded or used in production. Priorities may be linked to a quota system regulating the amount each legitimate demander or producer may receive. Quotas can alter the rule of how bids to buy or offers to sell are made. Finally, because allocation schemes and quotas often limit supplies in comparison to the unregulated market outcome, we expect a shift to less-competitive market rules.

Rationing may be performed in the distribution of goods and services using coupons or queuing. These methods are likely to alter supply and transaction rules dramatically, affecting not only who supplies, but how, where, and when transactions take place, and the transferability of property rights. An extensive system of rationing by queuing may even alter the medium of exchange, where money may be replaced by waiting time (Barzel, 1974). Efficiency in the allocations of the rationed goods may be preserved if secondary trade among individuals is allowed by the rationing rules (Sah, 1987).

The government may impose wage and price controls and then allow sellers to distribute their available supplies at the fixed price levels. With market structure rules, these controls will affect how offers to sell are made and how goods and services are priced. Where the government fails to set priorities for distribution, it is likely that the sellers will devise an allocation system of their own. For example, sellers may sell on the basis of first-come, first-served; established trading relationships; or only when monetary prices are supplemented with payments-in-kind (Jones, 1975).

Fiscal and Monetary Control

Selective intervention through fiscal policy probably is familiar to most government institutions operating under the conditions of the Bureaucratic Nightmare scenario. More generally, every level of government engages in fiscal policy of some kind to encourage certain economic activities and discourage others. In the recovery cases, we expect taxing and spending capabilities to exist in some operable form, although some adjustments to the system may be necessary. In development cases, efforts to influence supply and demand for essential goods and services may require the government to be in a position to affect prices through taxation, subsidization, and government procurement. Fiscal controls can be used to shift supply and demand, as well as alter production or consumption processes by the differential taxation of inputs or goods.

As a substitute for, or in agreement with, fiscal intervention, monetary policy may be used to remove purchasing power from demand. While purchasing power can be affected generally by monetary reform, selective reform can be used to direct resources into specific markets and away from others by altering the worth of particular asset types. Such a policy was followed in post–World War II Germany, where bonds and mortgages were revalued in the new currency at a higher exchange rate than the rate used for more liquid assets (Hill, 1987).

RECOVERING FROM THE BUREAUCRATIC NIGHTMARE SCENARIO

There are two circumstances in which it may be necessary to recover from the Bureaucratic Nightmare scenario itself. The first is where government intervenes excessively in its attempts at postdisaster stabilization and control, such that it actually displaces many of the free market institutions that initially survived the original disaster. The second circumstance is where central government intervenes for an excessive period of time, establishing bureaucratic agencies responsible for investment and wage, price, and production supply decisions. Here agency bureaucrats have an interest in maintaining control, and the population becomes increasingly reluctant to take the risks associated with market economy exchange. Some insights into the problems of transition from this fixation with the Bureaucratic Nightmare scenario can be gained by examining the emerging reports on democratization and free market liberalization of Eastern Europe.

It is worth beginning by summarizing the problems facing a centralized, planned economy where the political desire is to introduce a system of market exchange, and then going on to examine the problems that occur as the planned economy attempts to turn to private ownership and market structures. Poland, Hungary, Czechoslovakia, East Germany, Romania, Bulgaria, and Yugoslavia in 1989, and the Soviet Union in 1991, went through political transformations involving varying degrees of democratization and made differing progress toward economic privatization and laying the foundations of a market economy. Recognizing that each of these countries has its own historically unique problems, ethnic divisions, and different levels of industrialization, and that each began to reform at differing times and in different ways, it is still possible to identify certain common problems that these societies experienced in moving toward rules consistent with market structures.

Each society prior to transition had established a one-party Communist government and a legal structure that supported state ownership at the expense of private ownership. Prior to economic demonopolization, the state owned 95 percent of production outside of agriculture. Laws limited the access of any private entrepreneur to capital, labor, machinery, and raw materials. State industrial production units under the former Communist system were in the tens of thousand workers, whereas, at best, the private sector company was limited in size to, for example, five hundred workers in Hungary, or twenty workers in Yugoslavia (*The Economist*, 1989). In addition, the vast state-run companies were subsidized, and many operated at a loss. Price controls were such that state bureaucrats set most producer and consumer prices and made nearly all investment decisions because commercial banks did not exist. There were no stock markets because there were no private shareholders. The inefficiency of the command economy produced shortages for most basic food items, and there was a system of privileges and corruption whereby Communist Party members were able to obtain goods and services without standing in line. Every person was, however, employed even if underoccupied, and basic health care and accommodation was subsidized. Some of these East European nations such as East Germany had reached the top ten industrialized nations in the world, while others such as Hungary had a well-functioning market in food.

The introduction of economic reforms toward a market economy, most dramatically during 1989, meant that changes were necessary in all of these areas where, previously, intervention had been extensive.

Changes involving the withdrawal of government from economic intervention can neither happen instantly nor without high initial transition costs. It is one thing for the deputy prime minister of Poland's first non-Communist government to declare: "Our purpose is an economy based on market mechanisms, with a structure of ownership like that in developed countries; open to the world, its rules clear" (*The Times*, 1989: 11). But simply changing the laws, toward privatization of banking, credit, and allowing firms to freely compete does not alone guarantee that people will rapidly embrace the market system. In fact, the Eastern European case demonstrates that rather than encourage a reaction of enthusiastic entrepreneurship, radical changes in economic rules may elicit a response of "stunned apathy" (*The Economist*, 1989: 5).

In addition to the problem of apathy toward free market risk taking is the problem of the inflationary pressure that builds up in a system of government subsidies and price setting. Deregulating prices in a situation of shortages means massive price rises as can be witnessed in Yugoslavia, which, even before democratizing, freed its prices and experienced 1,000 percent inflation rate in mid-1989 that had risen to 2,000 percent by the end of that year (Trevisan, 1989: 7). Indeed, Poland, which was first to change to a non-Communist government but which was much later than Yugoslavia to move to a free market on pricing, began 1990 with the largest price increases in its post–World War II history. In that year, real living standards were expected to drop by 20 percent, with price rises for apartments, food, and fuel averaging 400 to 500 percent. By the end of 1989, the annual inflation rate for Poland was almost 900 percent. This contributed to bankruptcy, decreased production, and shortages, which caused further price rises (*The Times*, 1989). By the end of 1990 it had already brought a devaluation of the currency from 6,500 to 9,500 zlotys to the dollar. Similarly, in the phased introduction of free pricing in Hungary, which involved the withdrawal of large agricultural subsidies, the initial response was shortages and price rises (Beck, 1990). Recognizing the problems of transition cost and the concrete illustrations of the countries preceding them, has led the Deputy Prime Minister of Czechoslovakia to suggest that although they too will begin to tackle decentralization, the ending of state monopolies, the creation of capital markets, liberalization of prices and wages, and the liberalization of foreign trade, the Polish experience with hyperinflation showed that "such liberalization would have to proceed cautiously" (Lieven, 1989: 8).

There also are difficulties that arise when state enterprises are closed. Demonopolization through the withdrawal of subsidies means an initial rise in unemployment as inefficient government enterprises go bust. In Hungary, for example, the closure of fifty bankrupt state firms was expected to make 50,000 people unemployed (Beck, 1990). In Poland, about 400,000 employees were expected to lose their jobs during 1990 as the government closed inefficient companies (*The Times*, 1989). Until private entrepreneurs can make the product more efficiently at a price set by the market or until they can diversify into a product in demand, their initial departure will further fuel shortages, and thus add to price inflation, leading to further bankruptcies. Indeed, critical economic advisers to the Polish government have suggested that simply closing inefficient, state-run companies may be premature:

> Winding up uneconomic enterprises makes sense only when it is possible to transfer production to factories whose production costs are lower, which have spare capacity, the money to modernize or hard currency to import. In what name is the Government going to wind up a large number of enterprises which will be unable to cope with the rules of the market? In the name of what are we going to create 15 or 30 percent unemployment? ... The peril, in this view, is that Poland "de-industrializes," production drops and the country ends up with ... "more markets, fewer goods" (Boyes, 1989: 8).

Nor is the price-wage spiral weakened by government attempts to soften the impact of price rises and unemployment by increasing social welfare benefits, though clearly such measures will ease short-term political problems.

We see from this brief review of emerging developments that transition from the institution-intensive scenario of the Bureaucratic Nightmare to a market economy is itself something that needs to be planned for in advance, phased in rather than switched on, and that adequate time must be given for the market rules to develop and operate.

ACTIVITIES BEYOND GOVERNMENT REGULATION

In contrast to the situation of overcontrol already discussed, if government controls are not politically supported or are grossly inefficient, it is likely that trade for the essential commodities will be conducted in markets outside the legitimate or controlled structures. Depending on the level of resources devoted to monitoring and enforcing of the intervention controls and the level of resources necessary to evade the controls, informal markets in goods may arise that exhibit the rules characteristic of the associational market or the criminal variation of this market. Radford (1945) described the markets within a prisoner of war camp where exchange rules mimicking market activity were able to flourish in spite of the highly regulated atmosphere. Perhaps, even more dramatic are the numerous examples of colored or second economies of totalitarian Communist states (Grossman, 1977; Mars and Altman, 1983a; Sampson, 1987, 1988; Galasi and Sik, 1988).

Where government enforcement is lenient or monitoring of formal transactions, or activities, or both is very costly, associational market structures may arise to reallocate goods to more highly valued uses than would occur under the controlled mechanism. Where enforcement is strict or monitoring of formal activities very easy, trade in legal associational market structures will be too risky, and the criminal variation is a more likely outcome. Unlike the Business as Usual scenario, however, trade in Bureaucratic Nightmare informal markets is likely to occur at prices that are higher than the formal market prices, as economic agents attempt to obtain goods regulated by rationing or price controls.

This scenario concerns a world that is institution intensive relative to available, usable resources. We expect the associational markets, peasant marketplace, imperfect competition, oligopoly, and monopoly markets to be the primary exchange structures to evolve under these conditions. Exchange approaching the perfectly competitive market will be very unstable because of the high levels of uncertainty and the likelihood that it will be profitable for groups to form coalitions. Further, although imperfect competition may exist, it will be difficult to maintain without explicit government intervention to prevent mergers among suppliers.

FUNCTIONS

The Bureaucratic Nightmare scenario resembles Business as Usual in that it has an operating infrastructure. We examine in the following sections how the basic functions will be performed by the remaining institutions and exchange structures. The severe limitations on available resources to perform the necessary and facilitating functions for exchange in the Bureaucratic Nightmare scenario produce significant differences from the way they are performed in the Business as Usual scenario.

Define Property Rights

Court and regulatory systems define and enforce property rights in the Bureaucratic Nightmare for most of the formal-market transactions. Individuals are likely to seek coalitions with other property owners, however, because at the low resource level, property disputes may be expensive to settle in the court system and protection of these rights will also be costly. In illicit informal exchange, property rights are defined within the criminal market.

The government may use shared or common property rules to encourage an atmosphere of fair distribution as one way of establishing its authority position. This is particularly important where the population is making demands on the government to regulate the distribution of essential goods and services.

Convey Supply/Demand Information

In Business as Usual, prices or social networks largely performed this function. Given that prices may be either controlled or supplemented with payments-in-kind in the Bureaucratic Nightmare scenario, supply/demand information will have to be collected and distributed through other means. One source might be government sponsored programs similar to those used by the Cost of Living Council in the 1970s. Another source may be the increased network activity by market agents, especially where the rules of associational or peasant markets dominate exchange. Information reported through network ties or the visibility of displayed goods (or lack of them) for sale may act as a substitute for the formal price mechanism.

Provide Opportunity for Legitimate Transactions

To some extent the government will perform this function directly when it uses a rationing or other allocation mechanism to distribute goods and services. Where government regulation acts to create less competition among firms, the resulting market power may limit some of the transaction opportunities for demanders. In the informal exchange, the associational networks will serve to expand the trading opportunities among members.

Limit Provisions of Legitimate Contracts

Government can be expected to try to perform this function, but, with severely constrained resources, it may face enormous enforcement and monitoring limitations. Exchange structures may also provide rules that limit provisions; however, traders will face the same resource poor conditions as the government. Therefore, enforcement that cannot be implemented through network rules is not likely to be effective, and we should expect a much more vulnerable and perhaps illicit trading environment relative to Business as Usual.

Enforce Contracts Other Than by Physical Coercion

The desire for repetitive exchange will act to enforce contracts between traders in divisible, nonessential goods. Where there is infrequent consumption, the conventional solutions to poor sampling opportunities such as advertising and other informational services will be costly because communication resources are limited. Thus, the conditions are more likely to support nonmarket exchange rules to govern the enforcement of property rights. In previously formal markets, traders are likely either to look to the formal legal system to enforce contracts or to seek membership in a coalition to increase their market power.

Settle Disputes

To the extent that it is difficult and expensive to identify the parties involved in a dispute, the dispute will probably remain unsettled. The government may desire to demonstrate its willingness to settle disputes in order to avoid civil unrest. Traders that enjoy some degree of market power may settle disputes by renegotiating prices after the transaction is complete. Such actions favor the rules of less competitive market structures. Thus, we expect greater use of network ties or trade relationships among parties to avoid the risk of unsettled disputes.

Maintain Civil Order

This function will be carried out largely by the surviving government authority. In the peasant marketplaces, a market patron (e.g., a religious leader) may serve to maintain civil order in localized marketplaces.

Legitimate Other Functions

The government's authority to legitimate its control over other functions, including enforcement, pricing, and guaranteeing currency, will be a problem when this authority is not vested at the level of government that can use the scarce enforcement and monitoring resources efficiently. For example, a city government will not have the authority of the state government, which, in turn, does not have all the powers of the federal level. However, it may be efficient to transfer some authorities among the levels if lower levels of government are more able to monitor traders than higher levels. Even where the authority is vested with the efficient level of government, the authority must be supported generally by the population because of the lack of resources to coerce private behavior.

Guarantee Currency and Close Substitutes

The guarantee of currency is one function that may be challenged in the absence of public support for the government. As with the Business as Usual, the value of close substitutes for currency will depend on the primary markets for their exchange. These values may be distorted, however, by government interventions, especially if there is government confiscation of these resources.

Administer Distributive Justice

Where goods and services are rationed, distributed through allocation schemes, or where taxation is used to redistribute wealth, the government is engaging directly in distributive justice activities. The private sector may also engage in these activities within associational networks or by foregoing profit opportunities as in the case of the West Coast Gas Famine.

Monitor and Modify Operations in Response to Changing Circumstances

Programs that are directed by the governing authority to allocate scarce essential goods are likely to use command rules. The rules will not respond to changing demand and supply information any better than traditional rules of fixed allocation, unless additional mechanisms are simultaneously put into place. Markets where competition is limited also will be slow to adjust to changing market conditions because the threat of shifting market shares is not very great (i.e., conditions are more favorable to monopoly or oligopoly rather than imperfect competition). Exchange that is conducted through the associational markets is likely to be the most responsive to changing conditions where information about the changes can be observed and market power between buyers and sellers is more balanced.

Mitigate Risk

It is not likely that the formal market structures will be able to perform this function without government intervention. This follows from the lack of resource diversity and high levels of uncertainty. Market traders are not likely to have the options of using traditional mitigation mechanisms offered in the Business as Usual markets, such as diversification of resource holdings and insurance (Stiglitz, 1974). Risk mitigation can be performed by the strengthening of network rules, and thereby increase the importance of associational exchange or less competitive forms of the formal markets.

Exploit Comparative Advantage, Specialization, and Division of Labor

Because of the numerous causes of market failure in the Bureaucratic Nightmare scenario, it is unlikely that these functions will be performed effectively while resources are severely restricted. Furthermore, with severely restricted resources, poor product and service opportunities will limit the specialization of skills. Finally, these functions will be dampened by the effects of government control and direction in critical markets. Other than specific intervention by the governing authority, the rent-seeking behavior of market agents may fulfill this function. In other words, as agents attempt to form coalitions or networks to increase market power, they may also exploit labor specialization and comparative advantage.

Reduce Transaction Costs for Intertemporal or Interregional Transactions

Interregional transaction costs are normally reduced by the development of communication and transportation resources. Government investment often is required because of the public good characteristics of these services. Intertemporal transaction costs are likely to be high given the pervasiveness of uncertainty. Except for network transactions, credit is difficult to obtain from private lenders in the absence of government guarantees and subsidies.

CONCLUSION

The extra-market institutions play a more dominant and visible role in the Bureaucratic Nightmare scenario than under Business as Usual conditions. We expect a much narrower range of formal market structures to function in this environment because resources cannot support market diversity. Furthermore, the factors that commonly underlie market failure are pervasive in the Bureaucratic Nightmare conditions. These factors include information and transaction costs, externalities in consumption and production, extreme market power, and uncertainty. Finally, because we assume that the institutional infrastructure is largely intact, we expect groups of traders to place frequent demands on government institutions as a means of changing the distribution of extremely scarce resources.

In our discussion, we assumed that most trade operated under a largely private property system; however, governments facing such conditions often attempt to enforce common property rules to promote social cohesion among constituents or to enter the market directly as a quasi-public trader. Open access to property is only likely to exacerbate civil unrest and deterioration of confidence in the trading environment; thus, a development strategy may be pursued to localize property ownership through homesteading rules or landlord systems.

Currency functions well if traders see the government as a legitimate authority to guarantee its value. Continued credibility of the currency is more likely where it is sufficiently circulated and recognized by commercial agents. The encouragement of general credit is more of a problem because private traders may be reluctant to take even minor risks involving strangers.

The highly uncertain environment and drastic limitations on consumption and production possibilities act to increase the market concentration among consumers as well as among producers. Consumers will attempt to transact in associational markets to reduce transaction costs. Suppliers will seek mergers to reduce the uncertainty of input availability and output demand. Further, government monitoring and enforcement activities may actually encourage market concentration as suppliers seek to minimize the costs of compliance.

Establishing a credible position of authority is a significant and difficult task for the government in the Bureaucratic Nightmare scenario. In the presence of severely limited resources, governments have to rely on the support of the population to enforce authority over many critical functions or place an additional strain on resources to amass enforcement power. Without popular support, the environment could decay quickly into the conditions of the Wasteland scenario. Thus, responding to the political demands of the constituents to earn their support places significant constraints on the government's options in restoring economic activity or implementing development strategies.

9

Problems and Possibilities: The Real World Scenario

We have examined four hypothetical, extreme cases reflecting combinations of high or low resources and institutional development respectively. These scenarios are useful for investigating many of the core exchange issues under very different social and physical conditions. Until now, our analysis has been limited by the static environment of each scenario. In this chapter, we extend our interdisciplinary approach and consider what we learn from our extreme scenarios about the logical possibilities for the dynamic exchange processes of real world development.

First is the richness of understanding that comes with focusing on the transactional level of exchange rather than on a more general classification of economic activity. Using the insights from our interdisciplinary approach, we return to the debate regarding informal exchange activities in modern economies. Our contribution to the debate is to go beyond the simple dichotomy of formal and informal economies. We do this by considering how exchange rules emerge outside the official or formally sanctioned rule structures to meet the exchange needs and changing conditions of traders.

Second is a greater appreciation of the relationship between institutional conditions and the resilience or viability of different exchange structures given changing physical conditions. The scenario analysis of earlier chapters uses extreme assumptions to reveal the relative strengths and weaknesses of different exchange structures to sustain trade, rather than focus solely on the conventional terms of optimal or maximum growth. With this new foundation, we return to the contemporary problem of sustainable development for developed and developing economies.

EXCHANGE RESPONSES IN MODERN ECONOMIES

Activities conducted within market structures of Western economies account for only a portion of the economic exchange activity with a significant amount of economic activity occurring outside of these structures (Herzog et al., 1989; Smith, 1987). We showed in Business as Usual, however, that even in market structures trading activity is based on widely varying rules of exchange. Similarly, the mere fact that exchange is hidden or absent from formal accounting ledgers does not mean that it is essentially different from exchange that is part of the official record. We return to the debate regarding formal and informal economic activity and ask what our approach can contribute to these long-standing arguments.

In the beginning of this book, we argued that the simple dichotomy between formal and informal is inadequate for an analysis of economic activity. An approach based on the rules governing exchange transactions is more appropriate to understand the forces driving market and nonmarket phenomena, and, in particular, to understand the issue of making markets. The formal/informal dichotomy, within a rules framework, serves only to distinguish between the official rules (i.e., those that are prescribed by governing or regulatory institutions) and those rules that are descriptive of the actual options for exchange agreements.

What has come to be known as informal exchange is often excluded from the definition of official exchange because it looks different from the stereotype of market exchange. In many cases, informal trading arrangements go underground precisely because of their illegal nature.

The either illicit or illegal nature of the activity gives rise to a network of social support, skills, and secrecy. This network transforms what might otherwise be understood as market exchange into something having a different meaning to the participants. Illegality can induce changes that alter the transaction options and basis of the exchange.

In capitalist societies, an example of changing options is from rules that support market exchange activities to rules that are more network-oriented, such as in the associational or intimate exchange structures. (For example, associational rules are used for goods like Tupperware and Amway to improve market share in an otherwise highly competitive market.) In Socialist societies, however, the reverse is found to be true, such that the change is from exchange regulated by command allocations to hidden exchange transactions that are typically based on the rules of market exchange. Thus, activities making up nonmarket exchange structures are often the antithesis of those comprising market exchange structures. Where nonmarket exchange structures dominate the national economy, as in Socialist societies, it is typical to find that market exchange structures form the unofficial economic activity (Portes and Borocz, 1988; Łoś, 1990).

The informality characteristic of these activities is not the major organizing force; this remains the particular combinations of rules used to accomplish exchange. However, the examples illustrate the dynamic potential of exchange structures to meet the transaction needs of their members by providing alternatives to the official or traditional routes of trade.

In the industrialized West, intimate exchange structures often take the form of mutual aid, are governed by the rules of positive reciprocity, and are celebrated by ritual. In contrast, the intimate exchange networks in developing countries such as Chile, or Socialist countries like the Soviet Union (at least until the time of this writing) are often mechanisms for the inheritance of privilege. Similarly, in seeking to purchase items through associational exchange in the West, one expects to pay less than the formal economy market price; in Eastern Europe the expectation for participants to the second economy through associational structures has been to pay more than the price in the state economy.

While similar exchange structures are operating in the cases above, the outcomes vary according to the needs of the participants. Often, the official exchange rules and resource limitations define these needs; once again illustrating the interdependence of the formal and informal exchange structures. Over and above the various arguments about classifications, the formal/informal activity literature provides a limited but enlightening investigation into the mutual nurturing of market and nonmarket activities and exchange evolution.

Exchange Responses to Market Rules

The coexistence of nonmarket exchange activities and the market economy in Western industrial capitalist societies has a considerable history. Ditton (1977) has shown that as early capitalism developed from feudalism, definitions and boundaries were created that anchored the emerging society. For example, the newly emerging capitalist class changed what had previously been acceptable exchange practices, based on the principles of payments-in-kind, into illegal activity. Developing Marx's (1842) observations about the theft of wood, Ditton demonstrates that the extended package of common rights enjoyed by feudal tenants in England made a major contribution to household budgets. These common rights were stripped away, however, by the eighteenth- century Acts of Enclosure. Woodgathering, game rights, and grazing rights became the crimes of wood theft, poaching, and trespassing.

Eventually, the consumption of a part of one's daily labor was redefined as employee theft and embezzlement. Indeed, the new and continuing status of illegality meant that feudal exchange became more dependent on established relationships and social institutions of trust because anything less could risk the penalties of law.

Styles (1983) has shown that workers in the newly founded manufacturing industries of late seventeenth- and eighteenth-century England constantly borrowed, bartered, and sold small quantities of materials among themselves and that these were seen by workers as part of their traditional payments-in-kind. However, he says that, in spite of the insistence by some historians that one of the main tasks of capitalist development was to remove such payments, most employers were unwilling to eradicate perquisites permanently because they served a useful control purpose (Styles, 1983). Another reason for their persistence was as a foundation for legitimate market economy businesses. Indeed, some early capitalists began their market economy enterprises on materials acquired from associational exchanges that, as Styles (1983: 179) says, "was widely believed to be a very common route of entry into manufacturing for men with little capital."

Evidence on the development of capitalism in contemporary Third World countries also supports the argument of the interdependency between market and nonmarket exchange. Regarding labor resources (Hart, 1973), informal income opportunities comprise modes of earning a livelihood that lie outside the formal wage economy (Bryant, 1980). The labor arrangements that operate through informal transactions provide essential goods and services for the survival of the waged work force and have been described as a traditional mode of petty commodity production existing in conjunction with capitalism. The informal arrangements exhibit, however, the characteristics of nonmarket structures through rules that discourage orientation to the accumulation of wealth and rules that encourage an egalitarian organization of economic activity (Bremen, 1976; Davies, 1979).

Moser (1978) claims, however, that workers in the informal economy of Third World capitalist countries are no more than disguised wage laborers. He points out that their production is subject to control by industrial capital that sets the volume, type, and quality of the goods that are produced. But Gerry (1987) argues that the reality of small-scale informal economic activity and its nonmarket characteristics can only be understood in the relationship of informal activity to the historical cycle of boom and slump in the economy.

The logic of this argument is straightforward. In order to develop, capitalism needs to find labor at the lowest possible cost. The business cycle of boom and slump requires that a pool of surplus labor exists that is available in times of boom to be employed cheaply but that can be laid off in times of slump at little or no expense to the employers. The nonmarket exchange structures composing the informal sector of the Third World is, thus, the means whereby multinational capitalist corporations are able to maintain a marginal work force available for employment at the lowest possible cost. The informal sector provides a self-help network of support, a safety net for the poor that sustains them, at no extra cost, until formal economy jobs are available. Nonmarket networks thereby serve the social reproduction of the surplus labor force (Mingione, 1985).

Thus, not only is nonmarket exchange bound up with the generation of market exchange structures, but such structures of exchange provide a bedrock of stability for continuing market exchange activity. Indeed, the absence of nonmarket exchange structures would likely slow economic development and delay recovery from episodic slumps.

Importantly, in spite of the original economic needs of its participants, nonmarket exchange in the form of intimate exchange structures can be more social than instrumental, as has been demonstrated in the ethnographies of Stack, Lowenthal and Dow. Stack (1974), for example, describes how, among African Americans, the limited supply of finished material goods is perpetually redistributed among networks of kin in the community. Dow (1977) and Lowenthal (1975) describe networks of mutual aid and support that have been important mechanisms for social bonding among isolated urban ghetto dwellers. Lowenthal (1981) documents the reciprocal transactions in white, working-class communities that take place among kin and friends and promote support networks.

Nonmarket exchange structures continue to fulfill modern exchange needs in spite of market alternatives. A compelling reason for this is the changing structure of capitalist society. Modern market systems facilitate greater individual choice over living and employment options and transform traditional family and community relations. The kinds of exchange once exclusively defined as intrafamilial now bleed into the wider set of economic relations. In turn, weakening family and community bonds create a need for exchange where self-help and mutual aid are integral to the transaction (Katz and Bender, 1976; Robinson and Henry, 1977).

Production in the regular market is also facilitative of nonmarket exchange activity. When do-it-yourself tools are sold to consumers by hardware stores or when department stores sell food mixers and other household appliances, they are obviously expanding the capitalist system of production. Simultaneously, these goods contribute to nonmarket associational and intimate exchange structures in ways that are not the case when finished consumer goods dominate the economy (Burns,

1977). The phenomenal growth in home improvement in which 87 percent of the U.S. population participates (Herzog et al., 1989) relies on materials and tools, such as paint, paper, laminates, wood, power tools, stepladders, work benches, screws, and nails, produced in the formal market economy.

Indeed, even the aspect of criminal exchange that involves theft from the workplace can make a contribution to the formal market system. Criminal exchange may provide worker incentives (Dalton, M., 1964), improve employee morale (Zeitlin, 1971), and aid employers in their relations with labor. For example, Mars (1982) argues that a traditionally enjoyed covert reward, such as pilfering a certain amount from the company, allows workers to exert a degree of control over the fruits of their labor and reduces their sense of alienation in the workplace.

The unofficial rewards also operate as a nonmarket prestige exchange in many occupations, enabling workers to construct an unofficial social hierarchy based on who supplies and who receives such prestige goods. Mars cautions employers to take seriously the opportunities for such exchange opportunities inside employment. Limiting the illicit activity where it has been previously tolerated can increase withdrawals from work, which may include strikes, because the employees are losing much more than a little extra money. Mars suggests that managements need to consider whether or not informal economic activities underpin a chain of social obligation and reciprocity: "It is a short-sighted and short-term aim merely to bring wages up to the level of total rewards" (Mars, 1982: 207).

Exchange Responses to Extra-Market Rules

Increasing state bureaucracy regulating traditional family responsibilities, such as education, policing, and welfare provides further stimulus for informal activities. The transformation of market economies into mixed economies involving state intervention and a considerable redistributive economy, can shift the rules of market structures to the more protective networks of nonmarket arrangements.

The development of centralized government and state taxation policy plays a significant role in generating informal activity (Bawly, 1982; Feige, 1987). Gutmann, an advocate of laissez-faire market economy, claims that laws that define taxable activities, also define activities that can avoid tax liability:

> The subterranean economy, like black markets throughout the world, was created by government rules and restrictions. It is a creature of the income tax, of other taxes, of limitations on the legal employment of certain groups and of prohibitions on certain activities. (1977: 26)

He argues that the redistributive economy, the welfare state, and the growing employment protection or equality legislation actually create the grounds for capitalist employers to go outside the system to employ workers off-the-books. Clear advantages for an employer in taking someone "off-the-books" encourage covert labor arrangements and the same need for network restrictions found in employee theft. Indeed, in the manifestos of some radical libertarians an underground pursuit of "guerrilla capitalism" is the major way to evade taxes (Cash, 1984). High taxes and increased welfare budgets provide a fertile environment for intimate or associational rules that protect noncompliance behavior.

The pursuit of political objectives may also facilitate the growth of informal activities and nonmarket rules. Weiss (1987: 218) argues that "the underground economy appears less as a phenomenon of crisis than as a political creation, in a sense that its conditions of existence—as a pervasive, routine and institutionalized presence—are significantly shaped by the state." She claims that the reportedly high level of underground economic activity in Italy can be traced to a number of state policies. For example, succeeding Italian governments have fostered informal arrangements by giving small formal companies privileges. This policy encourages many small employers to keep part of their production underground in order to retain the privileges and benefits enjoyed by small firms.

The second or parallel economies of Socialist planned economies provide the strongest evidence of the capability of exchange structures to respond to extra-market rules. Here, however, the response is movement toward market rules in the informal or hidden economy; although network rules remain important (Katsenelinboigen, 1977; Alessandrini and Dallago, 1987; Łoś, 1990). In the Soviet Union, for example, underground economic activity is known as *rabotat nalyevo* which means "on the left." Often, short cuts and avoiding red tape, through a reliance on intimate exchange structures, is the only way to fulfill official economic goals. Research has shown that this oiling of the wheels is achieved by *tolkachi* who are fixers, employed by Soviet factories to bypass bureaucratic constraints and to overcome shortages through an informal network of contacts (Mars and Altman, 1983a, 1983b; Sampson, 1987). Indeed, it was said of the pre-perestroika Soviet economy that the second economy

> serves the function of lubrication of the joints of a creaking system. It conduces to social stability by a reciprocal latent blackmail . . . the second economy in the Soviet Union is not only a frequent event, but pervasive; not only pervasive but routine; not only routine but planned for by the regime. (*U.S. Select Committee*, 1980, as cited by Pahl, 1984: 115–16)

It has taken more recent commentary to point out that under state socialism economic activity hidden from the state has different characteristics from its market economy counterpart. For example, in the second
economy, informal exchange "provides an 'escape valve' and a means
to circumvent supply bottlenecks in rigidly planned economies" and it
"represents a means of personal resistance to the existing political order
. . . it creates an avenue for civil society to manifest itself as distinct from
the state, thus offering a short-term and individualistic, but nevertheless
real, alternative to a politically controlled planned command economy"
(Portes and Borocz, 1988: 26).

Indeed, over and over the centralized system involving state planning
of the economy is held to be the cause of the emergence or growth of
the second economy. Hidden exchange structures characterized by market rules overcome administrative and bureaucratic inefficiencies that
lead to shortages of labor, goods, and services (Łoś, 1990).

We also note that these activities do more than respond to state central
planning, indeed, as in Cuba, they may have existed in relation to prior
regimes. But when the state replaces former powers, whether dictator-
ships or colonial ones, traders may seek the second economy networks
within the cracks of the new state order to fulfill their exchange needs.
As Łoś says,

> The second economy is not viewed merely as a response to the problems
> or contradictions within the first economy; it is also believed to be an
> important force contributing to the successive transformations within the
> first economy. (1990: 199–200)

At the transaction level of exchange, network rules act to protect
traders from problems as diverse as the loss of social bonding or the
discovery of participation in outlawed activities. As a first step, we have
emphasized how the dynamics of exchange structures work to offset
formal rules within a local or national economy. These dynamics are
largely driven by the disaggregated but similar needs of the trading
participants. In the next section, we consider an international setting
and how the exchange structure approach can contribute to possible
responses for sustainable development.

SUSTAINABLE DEVELOPMENT REEXAMINED

Exchange evolution, even in the Business as Usual case, is more than
a linear path to greater and greater use of market rules and institutions.
Our last discussion highlighted the balance between market and nonmarket exchange structures to provide services that support civil interactions.

Beyond exchange evolution is the question of viable development paths for societies with different combinations of institutions and resources. We observed in chapter 1 that the currently fashionable solution to development problems is *sustainable development*. We reexamine the sustainable development question in light of our approach to rules and exchange structures. To begin, we consider how others have defined the sustainable development approach.

The Bruntland report (World Commission on Environment and Development, 1987: 43) defines the sustainable development approach as, "development that meets the needs of the present without compromising the ability of future generations to meet their own needs." However, beyond this broad definition it is always difficult to pin down the advocates of sustainable development on what exactly the concept means and how we should make practical decisions about which development paths are actually sustainable (Brown et al., 1987).

The fundamental weakness of almost all existing approaches is the underlying assumption that the development and environment problem is one of optimizing resource use (Redclift, 1988). Indeed, Bruntland (1987) elaborates on the general definition of sustainable development as containing two key concepts: (1) needs, particularly needs of poorer groups and countries; and (2) limitations, particularly constraints implied by technology and social organization on the environment's ability to meet present and future needs.

Advocates of sustainable development in general want us to preserve species, avoid land degradation, prevent pollution, and achieve optimal allocation of water and other resources, but most of the policy instruments they choose seem to lead to greater anonymity among traders (an institutional rather than a resource issue). This is because sustainable developmentalists persist in seeing the issue as a technical one of satisfying demand with limited resources, in other words, as a resource issue and not as an institutional issue.

We suggest that the central problem of sustainable development is not a technical issue of satisfying demand but an institutional problem of restoring to economic actors consciousness of the consequences of their actions. In other words, our analysis leads us to suggest that sustainable development is not a problem of optimization of resources but of the balance of institutions and resources (which were the two variables we used to define our scenarios). Viewed in this way, sustainable development becomes a problem tractable principally at the transaction level at which our analysis operates and at which, we might claim, history is made.

This focus on the transaction level provides the solution to the question we raised in chapter 1, "how can the concept of markets help us to articulate the connections between local and global thought and action?"

We recognize that the increasing anonymity of regulatory and formal market responses may compound rather than alleviate pressures on the global environment. We are also forced, however, to reject the utopianism of localized voluntary frugality in an increasingly interdependent world. In chapter 1 we also recognized the superiority of market systems at providing societal wants. We are not ready to reject such a powerful mechanism for human development. But then we must ask what alternatives are available to the conventional strategies of managerialism (through bureaucracies or markets) on the one hand and collectivist utopianism (practicing frugality) on the other?

Our answer to this question is to look to the exchange structures and the ideal typical scenarios based on extreme combinations of resources and institutions. We would ask what elements of market and nonmarket exchange can be nurtured to optimize the economic efficiency of formal markets with the social effectiveness of networks. While markets provide goods at lowest cost, networks remind members of their mutual interdependence and the dependence of the whole on the natural environment and resources.

Institutional Failures of Existing Systems

Recent media attention has focused on the spectacular failures of Eastern European and Soviet economies, while the periodic incidence of natural disasters in developing countries highlights the institutional weaknesses of southern economies. Even the wealthy West has little grounds for smugness. All three economic systems appear to suffer from serious failures in providing both economic satisfaction and environmental security for their populations.

Despite the reassurance of economic resilience provided by the Business as Usual scenario, Western formal market systems present a problem for sustainable development. We argue that the problem is their emphasis on the anonymous satisfaction of anonymous demand and their blindness to the role of intimate, associational, and prestige institutions with respect to either the shaping of demand or the choice among alternatives for satisfying it.

If exchange in the official markets of Western economies is characterized by problems of increasing anonymity of the market institutions, exchange in Eastern European economies has been constrained by the anonymity of impersonal regulation compounded by chronic scarcity of goods and resources. This is a case of our Bureaucratic Nightmare scenario, although one in which it can be argued cogently that the shortage of resources was itself caused by the overdevelopment of controlling institutions.

Exchange in southern economies suffers from both institutional underdevelopment and resource scarcity. Much of the developing world, especially Africa, seems to resemble slightly less extreme versions of our Wasteland scenario. The primary resource constraints are development capital, indigenous technological capacity (especially trained personnel), and renewable raw materials such as fuelwood and potable water. Most nonrenewable or nonrenewed raw materials (such as minerals or tropical hardwoods, respectively) are exported to maintain the meager capital inflows required to support local elites. While exports of manufactured goods have increased from 13 percent of Third World exports in 1960 to 54 percent in 1982 (Bruntland 1987), the development of export manufacturing has been uneven throughout the developing world and usually is achieved at very high cost to the environment.

Three Solutions: Rational Management, Internalizing Externalities, and Voluntary Frugality

Until very recently, the repertoire of solutions to the problems of west, east, and south consisted of "more of the same." The traditional response to the failure of "community control" (i.e., the moral force of social networks) has been to increase bureaucratic control to manage problems, such as development and environment. This was the path followed by the United States in blazing the trail for the rest of the world in attending to the environmental costs of unrestrained markets in the 1960s and 1970s.

Ironically, the regulatory solution to the anonymity of the market system is to create greater anonymity through rules imposed and enforced by distant bureaucracies with inadequate resources for enforcement. Rationing and permitting also suffer from anonymity. Ration coupons can be traded, stolen, or forged. Black markets arise. Planned allocations are not realized. Free market critics of environmental regulation have been quick to connect the high cost and disappointing results of regulation (e.g., Superfund, OSHA, etc.) with the catastrophe of Eastern European economies.

The regulatory approach essentially is one of rational management of resources. As such, it fits neatly into the tradition of resource conservation for human use that was embodied in the person of Gifford Pinchot (first head of the National Forest Service). Pinchot's split with John Muir (founder of the Sierra Club) over the grazing of sheep in federal forest reserves symbolizes the most persistent cleavage within twentieth-century U.S. environmentalism—that between resource conservationists and radical preservationists (Nash, 1967). While conservationists were concerned with the planned use of resources, the preservationists sought to safeguard the aesthetic and spiritual values of nature from the hands of humankind.

In contrast to both the rational regulators seeking resource conservation and the preservationists advocating voluntary frugality (who at least agree that unrestrained market economies lead to environmental degradation), economists tell us that the problem of pollution in Western economies is not a consequence of a market industrial system but of the incomplete application of market principles (Montgomery, 1972). If the price was right, producers and consumers would not squander energy and other resources. If polluters were required to pay the true social and environmental costs of their discharges, then markets could be the instruments of efficient emissions reductions. We are told that the same principles of pricing are the key to environmentally sound development in the south also. Developing countries will achieve the "environmental transition" by growing their way to the era of postindustrial plenty.

When pushed beyond the level of a mere slogan, sustainable development usually comes down to the traditional philosophy of managerialism modified by a preference for market instruments rather than direct regulation. As such, sustainable development really is an Hegelian synthesis of traditional resource conservation and its more recent economic critique.

The modern preservationist solution to the problems of development and the environment is to limit growth through voluntary frugality. This solution corresponds in important respects to a voluntary imposition of the Fat of the Land scenario, in which plenty is achieved through the restriction of wants. That scenario teaches us, however, that the solution of restricting wants is only possible within close knit networks. The readjustment of consumption and voluntary simplicity advocated by preservationists (now often called "deep ecologists") is highly intractable, except among societies with low anonymity (e.g. Amish, Bushmen, etc.).

Hence, at one extreme, rational managers seek to create rules or change prices to regulate behavior. Our analysis of informal exchange structures shows us people's propensity to get around these policy instruments, however. Monitoring compliance and preventing cheating will be a problem, particularly for the Bureaucratic Nightmare and the Wasteland situations that lack resources to invest in monitoring and enforcement.

At the other extreme, preservationists seek to alter preferences and thereby change demand. We know that this only works under exchange arrangements that are highly personal, however. Our identification of nonmarket exchange structures and our scenario analyses indicate that the preservationists are right insofar as their preferred solution identifies anonymity as the problem of market systems and bureaucracies. Environmental degradation is not merely the consequence of industrial activity. It is a result of the alienation of human actors from the consequences of their actions. If Bennett (1976) is correct that man's use of nature is inextricably intertwined with man's use of man, we can see that the need facing Western market systems is for institutions to guarantee recognition of the interdependence among people and between human economic and natural environments. Therefore, a common facilitator for either rational management or preservation approaches is making the trader less anonymous.

Prices and Networks as Instruments of Change

Currently, popular solutions to so-called market failures (such as emission permit markets or other price mechanisms) lead to greater anonymity rather than connectedness. As such, they may prove to be as self defeating as the rational regulatory approaches they seek to replace. Simonis (1990) criticizes the belief that harmony between economy and ecology can be achieved by viewing complex industrial systems as self-contained entities.

Changes in tobacco consumption and smoking behavior in Europe and the United States during the past two decades illustrate our argument that pricing is not necessarily the primary instrument of behavioral change. Cigarettes in the United States are probably among the cheapest in the world, certainly in relation to income. Yet, during the past twenty years, especially in the last decade, U.S. smoking habits have changed beyond recognition. Although consumption among women has risen, overall consumption has dropped and smoking in public places is now the exception rather than the rule. These changes have not occurred because of top-down regulation and certainly not through pricing cigarettes in the direction of reflecting the huge social cost of smoking. Rather, the source of change has been peer pressure operating through social networks. This is the case both for increased cigarette consumption by women and the reduction in public smoking. On the other hand, in Britain and Western Europe, which are characterized by high tobacco taxes, smoking remains widespread. One can search in vain for non-smoking sections of restaurants or pubs. The smoke-free workplace is a rarity. We argue that, on this issue, Americans have been more successful than Europeans at overcoming the anonymity of the marketplace and establishing the connection between "man's use of nature" (tobacco and health) and "man's use of man" (the mutual accountability of members of social networks).

The European and U.S. positions appear to be more consistent with the price-is-right hypothesis if we turn to the issue of gasoline consumption. Due to taxation, gasoline prices in Europe are more than double those of the United States and, indeed, European vehicle fleets historically have achieved better gas consumption than in the United

States, ride sharing is more common, and people make more use of public transport. This, however, has always been the pattern of behavior in Europe. Gasoline taxes are an accepted means of raising government revenues and have always been fairly high. High-priced gasoline was not introduced *de novo* as an energy saving strategy in Europe. Private cars remained a luxury much longer than in the United States, and ride sharing was part of the web of community social obligations. Hence, even this case does not provide the evidence required to establish the dominance of price over social bonding as a driver of consumer behavior where markets do not consist of wholly anonymous traders.

Education and information is another variable and potential policy instrument to be taken into account alongside price and peer pressure. It does not, however, seem to be the determining variable in the smoking case. Expenditures on health education and government information programs on smoking and health have been extensive in Britain and some other European countries, but information alone seems to make little dent in the behavior of anonymous actors. Most information programs assume individual consumers making personal optimization choices in the marketplace. Yet again, there is evidence that the key factor in whether information alters consumer behavior is the route by which it is transmitted. For example, Kunreuther (1978) showed that the determining variable in whether consumers purchased disaster insurance protection was personal acquaintance with someone else who had it. The implication is that information and prices can influence behavior, but that the biggest changes in behavior result when price and information signals operate through interpersonal networks and not through the anonymous workings of the marketplace. Many other examples illustrate this point, including illegal drug use and drunk driving behavior.

The Moral Dimension

If prices and information provide only a partial explanation for changes and shifts in behavior, then what factors complete the puzzle? By looking at the extreme cases, our scenario analyses make a distinction between rules that promote individual anonymity and those that validate membership. For behavioral change that is consistent with sustainable development goals, we suggest that exchange in the official economies of the industrialized West may be too anonymous to be socially optimal.

The major financial market scandals of the past few years in both Britain and the United States have occurred precisely where traditional relationships relying on interpersonal trust have been replaced by anonymous trading relationships. Financial deregulation of the City of London has seen an end to the proud boast of the London Stock Exchange:

"My word is my bond." The junk bond kings of Wall Street would have had a more difficult time had they been subjected to the close personal scrutiny and potential sanctioning of a personalized financial community. The spectacular crisis of the U.S. savings and loan banks would not have been possible if the conditions of interpersonal scrutiny and trust portrayed in *It's a Wonderful Life* were a reality today.

We have already mentioned in chapter 2 that the world of Adam Smith was a world of highly developed civil society where the market was underpinned precisely by nonmarket networks that established relationships of trust and predictability of response. Many theorists do not seem to recognize that Smith assumed these kinds of relationships were necessary for the operation of socially optimal markets.

In one of the most radical conceptualizations in this regard, Etzioni (1988) has rejected the entrenched assumptions of the utilitarian, individualistic, neoclassical paradigm, pointing out that marketplace exchange is permeated with attempts not only to maximize self-interest but also seeking to do what is morally right. Moreover, he argues that humans' abilities to act rationally on their own as individuals advancing the self are affected deeply by how well they are anchored within a sound community and sustained by a firm moral and emotive personal underpinning.

The moral dimension of economic exchange changes our basic assumptions from those that neoclassical economics hold to be true for the official market system. For example, in their effort to measure the relative sizes of underground economies for different countries, Frey and Weck-Hanneman (1984) argue that in addition to the burden of taxation and of regulation, national tax morality significantly influences the size and development of the hidden sector.

According to Frey and Weck-Hanneman (1984), while high tax countries such as Sweden, Denmark, and Holland do have a relatively high level of hidden economy activity and low tax countries like Spain, Japan, and Switzerland have a relatively low level of hidden economy, this relationship does not hold true for all countries. Italy, for example, is a low tax country and has, on most estimates, one of the highest levels of hidden economy activity, which suggests that tax levels are not a sole determinant. This is explainable, however, by incorporating nonmarket economy social components, such as tax morality. When the fact that Switzerland has a high tax morality and Italy has one of the lowest is factored in, the variation in rankings becomes more understandable.

Prestige Exchange as a Policy Instrument

Our emphasis on the balance of resource and institutional constraints in sustainable development is a radical departure from the managerial approach of attempting to optimize resource use directly. It may lead us to reevaluate some conventional assumptions about human behavior and its effects on the environment. For example, prestige exchange is frequently associated with conspicuous consumption or the production of "positional goods" (Simonis, 1990) that is assumed to be wasteful of resources. Anthropologists have previously made the argument that conspicuous consumption in tribal societies may be a means of limiting human impacts on the environment by periodically pruning the extent of human demands on renewable resources (Rappaport, 1968). Our analysis suggests, however, that the prestige economy could be extended as an instrument of environmental policy in industrial society also.

Firstly, prestige exchange systems develop close identification of actors and actions. The reputational dimension of prestige exchange can be applied to firms in industrial economies just as effectively as to individuals in traditional societies.

The use of prestige exchange to modify industry behavior is already a familiar device for many governments. Moral suasion is a recognized policy tool where the government uses threats to damage the reputation of firms and jawboning to influence business decisions (U.S. Department of Energy, 1989).

Moral suasion has the force of regulation without the need for formal legislation; however, there may be threats of informal sanctions. Jawboning is used where the government establishes "good" and "bad" behavior (Scherer, 1980). Federal guidelines for wage and price controls provide examples of jawboning policies. Firms that are targeted by a jawboning campaign will face rewards commensurate with their cooperation. An even more aggressive approach to persuasion and behavioral change occurs where the government discloses specific information to enhance or damage a firm's reputation.

We have argued that under different scenarios of resources and institutional development, prestige exchange is the basis of healthy credit systems and institutional trust. These outcomes are likely to be important components of new institutional arrangements, such as emissions trading or pollution permits. Firms that have earned high prestige can be allowed to borrow environmental quality because they can be relied on to pay back at high "interest" (positive reciprocity). On the other hand, firms that perform badly in the prestige economy are likely to require more restrictive regulation and be permitted less market flexibility.

Understanding the exchange structures that rely on intimacy, networks, trust, and so on is important in that it may correct our tendency to seek policy instruments for sustainable development among a limited range of increasingly anonymous mechanisms aimed solely at resource use.

CONCLUSION

The real world challenges us to consider the evolutionary properties of exchange rules and institutions. Unlike the scenario analysis, the real world contains a spectrum of resource and institutional combinations. We have highlighted a number of real-world problems for which our interdisciplinary approach provides an alternative to the conventional view. Making markets is sometimes an appropriate evolutionary response to satisfy the wants of society. The problem of sustainable development reminds us, however, that unbridled market development is hardly a social optimum.

Nonmarket and market structures not only exist simultaneously but seem to work together to provide an overall balance for the trading environment. We have argued that the complementarity is observed as an evolutionary response to meet the needs of traders. This response may arise to provide social connectedness or enlarge the trading opportunities where they are forbidden or hopelessly inefficient.

Our analysis of the complementarity of market and nonmarket structures challenges the conventional dichotomy of formal and informal economies. Other than distinguishing two economic sectors, this dichotomy fails to inform about the nature of exchange as it is conducted by participants.

We also identified networks as key factors in the dynamic responses of exchange structures. Networks are important in problems of social bonding, the protection of trading members, and the guarantee of social responsibility and accountability. Where informal economic activity also implies illicit or at the furthest extreme, illegal transactions, networks are integral to the hidden activity. As noted above, however, the market or nonmarket orientation of the informal sector depends on the orientation of the formal sector.

Finally, we extended the evolutionary focus to consider development and in particular, the problem of sustainable development. We argued that all too often, market rules are promoted by advocates of managerialism without careful attention to the full consequences of this advice.

Market rules, while promoting efficient and extensive opportunities for developing economies, also promote a high degree of anonymity among traders. Anonymity contrasts starkly with other social objectives that are important for the sustainable development problem, such as social connectedness and accountability. We suggested that nonmarket rules are worth considering where prestige and membership can be used as valued rewards in the exchange process.

10

Conclusions

The analysis in each of the chapters describing the four development scenarios indicates that not all exchange structures are expected to be stable in all environments. Table 2 summarizes the relationship between scenario conditions and stable exchange structures. Underlying the hypothesized stability of any exchange structure is a required consistency between the scenario conditions and the constitutive rules of the structure. Notwithstanding the dynamic considerations, our analysis has indicated that market exchange structures are more likely to survive and remain stable in those scenarios with higher levels of institutional development. The nonmarket structures are more dominant in the scenarios where institutions are virtually nonexistent or underdeveloped.

Consideration of the combination of rules vectors that constitutes the overall exchange process in each scenario yields a range of tentative conclusions. Of particular significance are the definition of property rights; currency versus barter, including problems of credit; demand and supply, including changing wants; modes of production, including the division and scale of labor; and issues of trust and authority. Additionally, it is appropriate to consider the routes by which exchange structures could develop towards a sustainable system that satisfies the conditions necessary for subsequent economic growth and technological development.

Table 2
Exchange Structures Combine Differently in Each Scenario

	Scenario			
Exchange Structure	Business As Usual	The Wasteland	Fat of the Land	Bureaucratic Nightmare
Nonmarket				
Subsistence		X	X	
Prestige		X	X	
Intimate	X	X	X	
Market				
Peasant		X	X	X
Associational	X	X		X
Criminal	X	X		X
Perfect Competition	X			
Monopoly	X	X		X
Imperfect Competition	X			X
Oligopoly	X		X	X

PROPERTY RIGHTS

Our examination of the four development scenarios indicates the importance of establishing property rights for development of a sustainable system of production and exchange. Prescriptions to maintain established property rights need to be tempered, however, by consideration of the level of development for both resources and institutions. Our examination of property rights at different levels of development indicates that, at low levels of institutional development (i.e., the Wasteland and the Fat of the Land scenarios) specific property rights will not be definable by centralized policy but will emerge from the necessity of available goods combined with the particular vision of distributive justice that predominates among the population.

In times of crisis, private property owned by anonymous shareholders (e.g., corporate property or unclaimed lands) is likely to be a prime candidate for redistribution. We see this reflected both in pressures for land reform and population resettlement policies in Latin America. In contrast, a community's common knowledge of the ownership of lands and homes by identifiable individuals probably will be respected. Under Wasteland conditions, however, even if there is a desire to maintain established property rights, the weakness of currency and the whole structure of financial debt lead to serious and widespread disputes about the just allocation of real property. The inadequacy of record keeping, such as land registries, mortgage records, vehicle and boat registries, and banking records, makes settlement of disputes all the more difficult as would the absence of consensual authority to adjudicate.

Even in the Bureaucratic Nightmare scenario, the governing authority might do best by not supporting all existing private property rights. Long-term development might be better served by the avoidance of civil unrest and the promotion of social bonding through partial compensatory reallocation on deep-pocket principles or participation in newly established or prevailing common property rights. Common property rules may create the incentives for individuals to act in the interests of the whole. Such actions might follow from the need for the government to demonstrate a response to the demand for public intervention to regulate market activities, especially where these bring severe hardship to some sectors of the population.

A common property system makes fixed allocations of goods and services to individual and group members. Efficiency may still be promoted under a common property system as long as transferability of these individual shares is preserved. By displaying fairness in the initial allocations at the beginning of the production/consumption process, however, rather than through redistributive activities at the end of it, the rule makers demonstrate a commitment to equity during the critical early period of development. Over time, as the fairness of the exchange environment and trust in trading partners is established, the environment is more conducive to exploiting gains from trade and the establishment of greater individual control over resources.

CURRENCY VERSUS BARTER

Prior analyses have argued that the establishment of a viable currency is a priority for development in order to avoid the inefficiencies of barter. In this respect, they share the prejudice that barter is necessarily less efficient than currency because it imposes high transaction costs. These costs arise from the need for traders to negotiate face-to-face and because information, in the way of a price signal, does not spread to the rest of the market. Furthermore, traders may not know what others desire, or there may be difficulties displaying and transporting goods for exchange. There are conditions where barter can be more efficient than cash transactions, however.

Where currency is in limited supply or has limited credibility but labor services are available, transaction costs will be lower if a trader can swap labor for goods directly, as in the Fat of the Land scenario. In other instances, barter may overcome informational inefficiencies in a changing environment. Where prices are established by customary allocation (as in the Wasteland) or by command levels, or simply take time to change (as in the Bureaucratic Nightmare scenario), traders may not have information on how demand and supply information changes. In these conditions, barter may encourage continuous transactions in an uncertain environment.

Centralized currency is entirely dependent on the credibility of the institution that underwrites it. No such institutional framework exists under the Wasteland or Fat of the Land conditions of development. In these cases, currency or close substitutes may emerge from a quite unexpected source. Specie money, like gold coin, may well derive from prestige exchange items that initially have fixed values in a restricted sphere, as in Kwakiutl coppers or Siane shillings. These scarce goods cannot be exchanged for what are considered commonplace or nonprestige goods; however, those that are durable act as a store of value. Those that are most liquid become exchangeable at traditionally fixed rates for all other prestige goods, though not for commonplace goods. Those that fulfill both conditions become specialized currencies within the prestige system.

True money, a general medium of exchange, may emerge in at least two ways. First, through an innovation in the rules that permits the specialized prestige currency to be exchanged for commonplace goods (e.g., gold). Second, through the introduction of a novel commodity that is not traditionally defined as either a commonplace or a prestige good (e.g., Western paper money in tribal societies) and can, therefore, be used as a medium through which both types of goods may be traded for each other. Such innovations may be the result of convenience or necessity.

We have seen that the prestige economy is inextricably linked to conspicuous consumption and, sometimes, the extravagant destruction of property. The delayed reciprocity characteristic of prestige exchange may be a precursor of credit. Credit is necessary for coordinating trading activities where sale and purchase are not spatially or temporally coterminous. The risk imposed on the creditor, who has restricted information on the debtor and limited opportunities for mitigation, is a powerful disincentive for the emergence of a credit market. An alternating balance of running debt is a powerful means of promoting social bonds between exchange partners, however. Prestige exchanges encourage this kind of risk taking between traders, who show off their status and wealth precisely by displaying how much they stand to lose if their partner defaults. At the same time, the action signals good faith and develops an atmosphere of trust as well as rivalry. As the prestige network expands, the use of delayed reciprocity for prestige prestations may encourage a growing population of traders to extend credit in the nonprestige exchanges. This is yet another reason to be very careful in attempting to restrict nonessential trading and conspicuous consumption on the road to development.

DEMAND AND SUPPLY

Many studies addressing economic development assume that the objective of policy actions is the rapid implementation of the capitalist industrial system; however, our analysis indicates that more attention must be focused on the process of conferring value on goods in the development process.

First, in cases of restoration or dramatic economic change, there will be major shifts in supply and demand conditions. Resources to produce certain goods may become scarce, as in the Bureaucratic Nightmare or the Wasteland scenarios, or the ability of a good to satisfy the wants of demanders may be destroyed, as under Fat of the Land. Hence, the supply of some items previously in common use may become scarce and, thus, prohibitively expensive (such as communication services) or unusable (such as a tractor without gasoline or viable substitutes). In the first case, the good is very valuable; in the second it is not. Such changes in demand functions must be anticipated in preparing policies for the allocation of scarce resources in development, especially where missing markets for information prevent the planner from relying on price signals for guidance.

Second, because certain goods are unavailable, the uses to which they are put may systematically lose their attractiveness over time. This may occur in the Fat of the Land scenario as well as the low resource scenarios because the existing social structures may have a strong incentive to shape the utility functions of their members to promote social cohesion. Hence, rules may emerge to limit the disruption caused by expression of demands that cannot be satisfied. This socially modified demand function does not, therefore, rely on antitechnology or antiindustrial psychological reactions to development but on the need to maintain social order and exchange itself. These changes in demand function must also be anticipated in planning for sustainable development.

CHANGING MODES OF PRODUCTION

The scale and locus of productive labor may shift radically in emerging development markets. As diversity of labor expands, traditional rules

become less and less applicable to the choice of how income is earned
and what can be done with it. Thus, it is unclear whether diversity is
really an outcome of the market process or the stimulus needed to generate it.

The expansion of labor skills into specialized areas undermines a system of universal traditional rules. When everyone can do everything,
all possess the knowledge and means to regulate each other's behavior.
It is the expert who defies universal regulation, not only because he has
proprietary information, but also because every expert, by definition,
possesses some specialized skills not found in the average member of
society at large. Thus, many professionals and craftsmen are regulated
by their own professional groups or guilds, rather than by general labor
restrictions.

Labor specialization makes members of a social unit highly interdependent, hence more vulnerable to severe losses in the context of economic change. The absence of markets in the Fat of the Land scenario
and the absence of resources in the Wasteland inevitably will restrict
the available range of goods and services. The absence of specialized
labor and existence of a domestic mode of production, in turn, limits
further the incentives for market behavior and encourages reliance on
fixed rules of allocation.Therefore, it may be very difficult for potential
middlemen to ignite true market activity.

TRUST AND AUTHORITY

A pervasive problem facing all traders and decision makers in the face
of rapid economic development is the issue of trust. In scenarios with
low development of institutions, licensing, certification, and consumer
rights, authorities will be severely restricted, if they exist at all. People
will experience difficulty in deciding who has the skills that they ad-
vertise, as well as who will behave with fiduciary responsibility. The
closer society is to familiar circumstances, the more trust will be retained
by existing institutions.

Even under the conditions of Bureaucratic Nightmare, however, institutions will have to exercise great care in the planning and execution
of policy. For example, failure to respond to popular demand for regulation under conditions of high institutional infrastructure and low
resources may well compromise the government's authority as an equit-
able decision maker, capable of guiding development. Equally danger-
ous would be the tendency to regulate and even eliminate exchange
activities that might make a valuable, if not always obvious, contribution
to the development of currency, credit, and social cohesion.

One of the more critical problems to be faced by developing institutions will be the maintenance of authority. This will be exacerbated

where resources are underdeveloped but demand stimulated, because the institutions will not be able to sustain long-term compliance through physical or material coercion.

Some argue that authority ultimately rests on the power to coerce. This view is certainly consistent with our description of the Wasteland. Analysis of the Bureaucratic Nightmare scenario indicates that authority may stem equally from consensus about fixed allocations, where the patterns of exchange incentives are structured so as to promote social bonding. Under these conditions, the decision maker may be faced with a trade-off between promoting competitive incentives for allocations to encourage middleman activity and maintaining the stability of civil society.

Where institutional infrastructure is largely undeveloped, especially as in the conditions under Fat of the Land, the emergence of prestige exchange may prove to be an important substitute for formal regulation, replacing legal sanctions by moral sanctions and possible loss of face. We argued in chapter 2 that civil society, based on interpersonal trust and regulated by traditional ethics, was the condition for the emergence of the modern market system. In chapter 9 we identified the societal consequences of the decline of trust and the interpersonal networks that are symptomatic of the increasing anonymity of competitive market structures.

THE SHIFT FROM NONMARKET TO
MARKET STRUCTURES

Having considered some of the conclusions from the static analysis of the scenarios, we can also suggest some propositions about the dynamic features of economic development. Our scenarios can be seen as starting from a Wasteland system of low resources and low institutional development that eventually moves to greater economic flexibility either through greater resource accumulation or institutional development. Thus, our Fat of the Land and the Bureaucratic Nightmare scenarios can be used as various pathways to the type of social organization that precedes the Business as Usual case.

Starting from the Wasteland, the presence of fixed rules of allocation within exchange structures may largely be responses to the severe transaction costs implied by initiating and completing exchanges. These rules will limit exchange opportunities by restricting permissible choices among traders. Thus, these rules may be an impediment to the development of a market process.

On the other hand, the traditional rules encourage activities that are necessary precursors to many social functions that constitute formal market structures. These activities include delayed reciprocity and the extension of credit; definition of property rights; signaling of good faith and credibility; and demonstration of sanctions for rule violations. We argued in chapter 9 that interdependencies between market and non-market exchange structures provide mutually supporting conditions. Interdependencies encourage the development of credit and currency systems, an atmosphere of trust, and contract compliance among traders and, thus, contribute to continued market evolution.

To have truly a market process, however, the rules of fixed allocations must begin to be superseded by rules that extend the transaction choices available to trading agents. Innovation in the rules leading to greater flexibility may be stimulated by either internal or external conditions, always present in a changing social and physical environment. Increases in the division of labor may be one such condition, contact with another exchange structure may be another. More generally, innovation in an exchange structure results from the changing needs of trading members, sometimes to seek alternatives to limiting or prohibitive rules.

Flexibility in the Wasteland system increases with greater resources (and less violent competition for basic survival) and greater institutional development as exchange relationships are fostered by greater control over civil actions. Flexibility promotes the opportunity to exploit gains from trade and contributes to a higher mobility of resources among traders and with other exchange structures.

Flexibility is essential to the rules of the competitive market structures. We cautioned in chapter 9, however, that unbridled market development has serious consequences for nonefficiency societal goals. Sustainable development demands a balance between anonymity in market trans-actions and social accountability for exchange activities. We suggest that solutions to achieve this balance may be found in the network rules of the nonmarket structures.

FURTHER RESEARCH

The topics explored in this book suggest a number of areas that warrant further research to understand better the implications of alternative policy prescriptions for economic development. Our analysis is exploratory, in the sense that it seeks to highlight the logical possibilities for exchange activities and then investigate the rules under which these activities may transpire. As a result, our analysis points out specific questions regarding exchange activity and economic recovery that must be investigated in a more narrowly focused analysis.

Three topics that require more investigation for policy purposes are property rights, currency versus barter, and trust and authority. We find these topics to be central concerns in each of the scenarios. We recommend that a more focused analysis of each topic be undertaken to provide the basis for concrete policy recommendations.

Two aspects of the problem not addressed by our study are the macroeconomic effects and the international implications of economic development. In order to assess the potential routes of economic development fully, a complementary understanding of these various perspectives is required.

At a more microlevel of analysis, further insight on development options could be gained by empirically testing the behavioral responses of economic agents to changing economic conditions and rules governing exchange. This may be done using experimental economics techniques, where the behavioral responses of traders presented with various rules can be observed. Another possibility is to conduct field analyses of persons or groups that regularly engage in exchange activities that largely reflect the dominant rules of one or another of the exchange structures outlined in our study. This would allow a more detailed understanding of how people actually react to the exchange rules they face.

While our study does explore some aspects of the relative resource and institution development, more detailed aspects could assist in fine tuning policy prescriptions. For example, in the Bureaucratic Nightmare scenario we look at a world where it is assumed that it is largely government institutions that provide the engine for change and development. Thus, our scenario suggests a world that has a large public sector relative to the private counterpart as has been the case historically in the Soviet Union and Eastern Europe. Similarly, the Fat of the Land scenario assumes a world where agricultural and extraction resources are plentiful relative to other resource types. This could be extended to explore different public and private sector and resource relationships by using a comparative regional model to identify scenarios involving variation in regional development.

Finally, an important issue for further study pertains to the dynamic properties of exchange structures. Specifically, we encourage more consideration of how market activities may be managed to evolve from structures that are characterized by fixed rules of allocation. Our study hints at a possible progression from fixed allocations to market activities when old rules are superseded by rules that extend the available transaction choices. Nonmarket and market structures are, however, mutually dependent in this evolution. In the case of Western industrial economic evolution, this process took several hundred years. Thus, questions remain unanswered regarding the dynamic possibilities under conditions of rapid economic development as are currently being experienced in Eastern Europe and the Soviet Union. A logical next step in the research is to explore to what extent explicit policy actions, rather than time and the demands of disaggregated traders, could be used to circumvent or hasten the evolution of exchange structures to produce desired economic systems.

MAKING MARKETS: A COMPARATIVE
INTERDISCIPLINARY PERSPECTIVE

We began this book by recognizing the limitations of single disciplinary perspectives in addressing the problems of sustainable economic development and noted at the outset the absence of a definition of the market. In one sense our whole book has been an attempt to provide an interdisciplinary definition of the market and to elaborate this through the constitutive analysis of a series of ideal type comparative scenarios. We believe that such an approach transcends the limitations of any one discipline, because it is capable of capturing the microparticularistic and the macrogeneral levels of market process. While a critical evaluation might suggest that we have done little more than provide a typology of market structures, such a view misses the importance of the comparative microeconomics that our analysis is designed to illustrate. We have generated an analytical framework that is founded on a rules-based approach to the constitution of various aspects of exchange activity. As an initial statement, this book presents a comparative analysis of hypothetical scenarios and market-making behavior. Ultimately, its value will depend on refinement of the concepts for real world conditions to support the policy makers of developing economies, changing economies, and destroyed economies, all of whom are confronted by the problem of making markets.

References

Alchian, A. A., and W. R. Allen. (1969). *Exchange and Production: Theory in Use*. Belmont, Calif.: Wadsworth.

Alessandrini, S. and B. Dallago, (1987). *The Unofficial Economy: Consequences and Perspectives in Different Economic Systems*. Aldershot, U.K.: Gower.

Arrow, K. J. (1969). "The Organization of Economic Activity: Issues Pertinent to the Choice of Market Versus Nonmarket Allocation." In *The Analysis and Evaluation of Public Expenditure: The PPB System*, vol. 1. Washington, D.C.: U.S. Government Printing Office.

Arrow, K. J., and G. Debreu. (1954). "Existence of an Equilibrium for a Competitive Economy." *Econometrica* 223: 265–90.

Arrow, K. J., and F. H. Hahn. (1971). *General Competitive Analysis*. San Francisco: Holden Day.

Aumann, R. J. (1964). "Markets with a Continuum of Traders." *Econometrica* 32: 39–50.

Bain, J. S. (1968). *Industrial Organization*, 2d ed. New York: John Wiley & Sons, Inc.

Barth, F. (1959). *Political Leadership Among Swat Pathans*. London: Athlone Press.

Barzel, Y. (1974). "A Theory of Rationing by Waiting." *Journal of Law and Economics* 17: 73–96.

Barzel, Y. (1982). "Measurement Cost and the Organization of Markets." *Journal of Law and Economics*. 25(1): 27–48.

Baumol, W. J., J. Panzar, and R. Willig. (1982). *Contestable Markets*. New York: Harcourt Brace Jovanovich.

Bawly, D. (1982). *The Subterranean Economy*. New York: McGraw-Hill.

Beck, E. (January 9, 1990). "Low Price Era Ends for Hungarians."*The Times*, 9.

Becker, G. (1976). *The Economic Approach to Human Behavior*. The University of Chicago Press.

Bell, D. (1981). "Models and Reality in Economic Discourse." In *The Crisis in Economic Theory*, D. Bell and I. Kristol, eds. New York: Basic Books.

Belshaw, C. S. (1965). *Traditional Exchange and Modern Markets*. Englewood Cliffs, N.J.: Prentice-Hall, Inc.

Bennett, J. W. (1976). *The Ecological Transition*. Oxford: Pergamon Press.

Benson, B. L., and M. D. Faminow. (July, 1986). "The Incentives to Organize and Demand Regulation: Two Ends Against the Middle."*Economic Inquiry* 24(3): 473–484.

Berenbeim, R. (1981). *Regulation: Its Impact on Decision Making*. Washington, D.C.: The Conference Board.

Blau, P. M. (1964). *Exchange and Power in Social Life*. New York: John Wiley and Sons, Inc.

Blau, P. M. (1968). "Interaction: Social Exchange." In *International Encyclopedia of the Social Sciences*, vol. 7. New York: Macmillan.

Bohannan, P. (1959). "The Impact of Money on an African Subsistence Economy." *Journal of Economic History* 19(4): 491–503.

Bohannan, P., and G. Dalton. (1962). "Introduction." In *Markets in Africa*, P. Bohannan and G. Dalton, eds. Chicago: Northwestern University Press.

Bott, E. J. (1957). *Family and Social Network: Roles, Norms, and External Relations in Ordinary Urban Families*. London: Tavistock.

Boulding, K. E. (1978). *Ecodynamics*. Beverly Hills, Calif.: Sage Publications.

Boyes, R. (December 13, 1989). "Poland and IMF Work Together to Build a New Economic System." *The Times*, 8.

Braithwaite, J. (1989). *Crime, Shame and Reintegration*. New York: Cambridge University Press.

Bremen, J. (1976). "A Dualistic Labour System: A Critique of the Informal Sector Concept." *Economic and Political Weekly* 11: 1870–76.

Brennan, G. and J. M. Buchanan. (1985). *The Reason of Rules*. New York: Cambridge University Press.

Brenner, R. (1978). "The Origins of Capitalist Development—A Critique of Neo-Smithian Marxism," *New Left Review*, 25–92.

Brenner, R. (1987). *Rivalry*. New York: Cambridge University Press.

Brown, B. J., M. E. Hanson, D. M. Liverman, and R. W. Merideth Jr. (1987). "Global Sustainability: Toward Definition."*Environmental Management* 11(6): 713–19.

Brown, R. M. (1979). "The American Vigilante Tradition." In *Violence in America*, M. D. Graham and T. R. Gurr, eds., pp.153–86. Beverly Hills: Sage Publications.

Bruntland, G. H., et al. (1987). *Our Common Future: Report of the World Commission on Environment and Development*. New York: Oxford University Press.

Bryant, J. (1980). "An Introductory Bibliography to Work on the Informal Economy in Third World Literature." In *Bibliographies and Local Labour Markets and the Informal Economy*, R. Pahl and J. Laite, eds. London: Social Science Research Council.

Burns, S. (1977). *The Household Economy*. Boston: Beacon Press.

Cantor, R., S. Henry, and S. Rayner. (1989). *Markets, Distribution, and Exchange After Societal Cataclysm*, ORNL–6384. Oak Ridge, Tenn.: Oak Ridge National Laboratory.

Cash, A. (1984). *Guerrilla Capitalism: How to Practice Free Enterprise in an Unfree Economy*. Port Townsend, Wash.: Loompanics Unlimited.

Chamberlin, E. H. (1956). *The Theory of Monopolistic Competition*, 8th ed. Cambridge, Mass.: Harvard University Press.

Cheal, D. (1988). *The Gift Economy*, New York: Routledge.

Cheung, S. N. S. (1983). "The Contractual Nature of the Firm." *Journal of Law and Economics* 26: 1–21.

Coase, R. H. (1937). "The Nature of the Firm." *Economica* 4(16): 386–405.

Coase, R. H. (1960). "The Problem of Social Cost." *Journal of Law and Economics* 3: 1–44.

Codere, H. (1950). *Fighting with Property*. New York: J. J. Augustin.

Coleman, J. W. (1989). *The Criminal Elite*. New York: St. Martin's Press.

Cook, K. S., R. M. Emerson, M. R. Gillmore, and T. Yamagish. (1983). "The Distribution of Power in Exchange Networks." *American Journal of Sociology* 89(2): 275–305.

Crémer, J. (1984). "On the Economics of Repeat Buying." *Rand Journal of Economics*. 15(3): 396–403.

Dalton, G. (1964). "The Development of Subsistence and Peasant Economies in Africa." *International Social Science Journal* 16(3): 378–389.

Dalton, G. (1982). "Barter." *Journal of Economic Issues* 16(1): 181–90.

Dalton, M. (1964). *Men Who Manage*. New York: John Wiley and Sons, Inc.

Davies, R. (1979). "Informal Sector or Subordinate Mode of Production? A Model." In *Casual Work and Poverty in Third World Cities*, R. Bromley and C. Gerry, eds. pp. 97–104. London: John Wiley and Sons, Inc.

Davis, J. (1972). "Gifts and the UK Economy." *Man* 7(3): 408–29.

Davis, J. (1973). "Forms and Norms: The Economy of Social Relations." *Man* 8(2): 159–76.

Debreu, G. (1959). *The Theory of Value: An Axiomatic Analysis of Economic Equilibrium*. New York: John Wiley & Sons, Inc.

de Chazeau, M. G., A. G. Hart, G. C. Means, H. B. Myers, H. Stein, and T. O. Yntema. (1946). *Jobs and Markets*. New York: McGraw-Hill.

Dennis, N., F. Henriques, and C. Slaughter. (1969). *Coal is Our Life*. London: Tavistock.

Ditton, J. (1977) "Perks, Pilferage, and the Fiddle: The Historical Structure of Invisible Wages." *Theory and Society* 4 (1): 39–71.

Douglas, M. (1958). "Raffia Cloth Distribution in the Lele Economy." *Africa* 28: 109–22.

Douglas, M. (1967). "Primitive Rationing." In *Themes in Economic Anthropology*, R. Firth, ed. London: Association of Social Anthropologists.

Douglas, M., and B. Isherwood (1978). *The World of Goods: Toward an Anthropology of Consumption*. New York: W. W. Norton.

Dow, L. M. (1977). "High Weeds in Detroit." *Urban Anthropology* 6: 111–28.

Durkheim, E. (1893). *De La Division du Travail Social* or *Division of Labor in Society* (trans. 1933). Glencoe, Ill.: Free Press.

The Economist. (August 12, 1989). "Eastern Europe." Special Survey Supplement.

Edgerton, R. B. (1985). *Rules, Exceptions, and Social Order.* Berkeley: University of California Press.

Eisenstadt, S. N., and L. Roniger. (1984). *Patrons, Clients, and Friends: Interpersonal Relations and the Structure of Trust in Society.* New York: Cambridge University Press.

Emerson, R. M. (1972). "Exchange Theory, Part I: A Psychological Basis for Social Exchange" and "Exchange Theory, Part II: Exchange Relations in Network Structures." In *Sociological Theories in Progress,* J. Berger, M. Zelditch, Jr., and B. Anderson, eds., pp. 38–87. New York: Houghton Mifflin.

Etzioni, A. (1965). *Political Unification: A Comparative Study of Leaders and Forces.* New York: Holt, Rinehart, and Winston.

Etzioni, A. (1988). *The Moral Dimension: Toward A New Economics.* New York: Free Press.

Evans-Pritchard, E. E. (1937). *Witchcraft Oracles and Magic Among the Azande.* Oxford: Clarendon Press.

Evans-Pritchard, E. E. (1940). *The Nuer.* Oxford: Clarendon Press.

Evans-Pritchard, E. E. (1951). *Kinship and Marriage Among the Nuer,* Oxford: Clarendon Press.

Faberman, H. A., and E. A. Weinstein. (1970). "Personalization in Lower Class Consumer Interaction." *Social Problems* 17(4): 449–57.

Faith, R. L., and R. D. Tollison. (1981). "Contractual Exchange and the Timing of Payment." *Journal of Economic Behavior and Organization* 1(4): 325–42.

Feige, E. (1987). "The Anatomy of the Underground Economy." In S. Alessandrini and B. Dallago, eds. *The Unofficial Economy: Consequences and Perspectives in Different Economic Systems.* Aldershot, U.K.: Gower.

Ferman, L. A. (1968). *Job Development for the Hard-to-Employ.* Ann Arbor: Institute of Labor and Industrial Relations, University of Michigan.

Ferman, L. A., and L. E. Berndt. (1981). "The Irregular Economy." In *Informal Institutions,* S. Henry, ed. New York: St. Martin's Press.

Ferman, P. R., and L. A. Ferman. (1973). "The Structural Underpinning of the Irregular Economy." *Poverty and Human Resources Abstracts,* 8: 3–17.

Filmer, P., M. Phillipson, D. Silverman, and D. Walsh. (1972). *New Directions in Sociology.* London: Collier-Macmillan.

Firth, R. (1951). *The Elements of Social Organization.* London: C. A. Watts and Co.

Forde, D. and M. Douglas. (1956). "Primitive Economies." In *Man, Culture, and Society,* H. Shapiro, ed. Oxford: Oxford University Press.

Frank, A. G. (1967). *Capitalism and Underdevelopment in Latin America.* New York: Monthly Review Press.

Frey, B. S., and H. Weck-Hanneman. (1984). "The Hidden Economy as an 'Unobserved' Variable." *European Economic Review* 26: 33–53.

Friedman, M. (1976). *Price Theory.* Chicago: Aldine Publishing Co.

Galasi, P. and E. Sik. (1988). "Invisible Incomes in Hungary." *Social Justice* 15: 160–78.

Garner, C. A. (1986). "Equity in Economic Relationships." *Journal of Economic Behavior and Organization* 7: 253–264.

Gaughan, J. P., and L. A. Ferman. (1987). "Towards an Understanding of the Informal Economy." *Annals of the American Academy of Political and Social Sciences* 493: 15–25.

Gerry, C. (1987). "Developing Economies and the Informal Sector in Historical Perspective." In *The Annals: The Informal Economy*,L. A. Ferman, S. Henry, and M. Hoyman, eds. Beverly Hills: Sage Publications.

Gershuny, J. (1983). *Social Innovation and the Division of Labour*. Oxford: Oxford University Press.

Gluckman, M. (1955a). *Custom and Conflict in Africa*. Oxford: Blackwell.

Gluckman, M. (1955b). *The Judicial Process Among the Barotse of Northern Rhodesia*. Manchester University Press.

Gould, J. (1980). "The Economics of Markets: A Simple Model of the Market-Making Process." *Journal of Business* 53: S167–87.

Gouldner, A. (1960). "The Norm of Reciprocity." *American Sociological Review* 25(2): 161–78.

Granovetter, M. (1985). "Economic Action and Social Structure: A Theory of Embeddedness." *American Journal of Sociology* 91(3): 481–510.

Gross, J. L., and S. Rayner. (1985). *Measuring Culture*. New York: Columbia University Press.

Grossman, G. (September/October, 1977). "The Second Economy of the USSR." *Problems of Communism* 26(5): 25–40.

Gudeman, S. (1971). "The Compadrazgo as a Reflection of the Natural and Spiritual Person." In *Proceedings of the Royal Anthropological Institute*. London.

Gutmann, P. M. (1977). "The Subterranean Economy." *Financial Analysts Journal*. 34: 26–27.

Hahn, R. W., (1989). "Economic Prescriptions for Environmental Problems: How the Patient Followed the Doctor's Orders." *Journal of Economic Perspectives*. 3(2): 95–114.

Hahn, R. and R. Noll (1983). "Barriers to Implementing Tradable Air Pollution Permits: Problems of Regulatory Interaction." *Yale Journal on Regulation*. 1(1): 63–91.

Hannerz, U. (1986). "Theory in Anthropology: Small is Beautiful? The Problems of Complex Cultures." *Comparative Studies in Society and History* 28(2): 362–67.

Hardin, G. (1968). "The Tragedy of the Commons." *Science* 162: 1243–48.

Harding, P., and R. Jenkins. (1989). *The Myth of the Hidden Economy: Towards a New Understanding of Informal Economic Activity*. Milton Keynes, U.K.: Open University Press.

Harris, M. D. (1940). *Two Famous Kentucky Feuds and Their Causes*. M. A. Thesis, University of Kentucky, Lexington.

Hart, K. (1973). "Informal Income Opportunities and Urban Employment in Ghana." *Journal of Modern African Studies* 11(1): 61–89.

Hart, K. (1986). "Heads or Tails? Two Sides of the Coin." *Man* (N.S.) 21(4): 637–56.

Haveman, R. H., and K. A. Knopf. (1966). *The Market System*. New York: John Wiley and Sons, Inc.

Heder, S. (1980). *Kampuchean Occupation and Resistance*. Bangkok: Asian Studies Monographs No. 027, Chulalongkorm University.

Henderson, J. M., and R. E. Quandt. (1971). *Microeconomic Theory: A Mathematical Approach*, 2nd ed. New York: McGraw-Hill.

Henry, S. (1977). "On the Fence." *British Journal of Law and Society* 4: 124–33.

Henry, S. (1978). *The Hidden Economy*. Oxford: Martin Robertson. Republished (1988) by Loompanics Unlimited, Port Townsend.

Henry, S. (1983). *Private Justice*. London: Routledge and Kegan Paul.

Henry, S. (1985). "Community Justice, Capitalist Society and Human Agency: The Dialectics of Collective Law in the Cooperative." *Law and Society Review* 19(2): 303–27.

Henry, S. (1988). "Can the Hidden Economy be Revolutionary: Toward a Dialectical Analysis of the Relations Between Formal and Informal Economies." *Social Justice* 15: 29–60.

Henry, S., and G. Mars. (1978). "Crime at Work: The Social Construction of Amateur Property Theft." *Sociology* 12:245–63.

Herskovits, M. J. (1962). "Preface." In *Markets in Africa*, P. Bohannan and G. Dalton, eds. Chicago: Northwestern University Press.

Herzog, A. R., R. L. Kakn, J. N. Morgan, J. S. Jackson, and T. C. Antonucci. (1989). "Age Differences in Productive Activities." *Journal of Gerontology: Social Sciences* 44: 129–38.

Hill, L. J. (1987). *Studies of Postdisaster Economic Recovery: Analysis, Synthesis, and Assessment*, ORNL–6230, Oak Ridge, Tenn.: Oak Ridge National Laboratory.

Hirshleifer, J. (December, 1985). "The Expanding Domain of Economics." *American Economic Review* 75: 53–68.

Hobsbawm, E. (1969). *Bandits*. London: Weidenfeld and Nicolson.

Holland, P. W., and S. Leinhardt. (1979). *Perspectives on Social Network Research*. New York: Academic Press.

Homan, P. T., and F. Machlup, eds. (1945). *Financing American Prosperity*. New York: The Twentieth Century Fund.

Homans, G. C. (1961). *Social Behavior: Its Elementary Forms*. New York: Harcourt Brace Jovanovich.

Homans, G. C. (1964). "Bringing Men Back In." *American Sociological Review* 29(5): 809–18.

Hostetler, J. A. (1963). *Amish Society*. Baltimore, Md.: Johns Hopkins Press.

Howson, G. (1970). *The Thief Taker General: The Rise and Fall of Jonathan Wild*. London: Hutchinson.

Hurwicz, L. (1973). "The Design of Mechanisms for Resource Allocation." *American Economic Review* 63: 1–30.

Illich, I. (1981). *Shadow Work*. London: Marian Boyars.

Jones, V. C. (1948). *The Hatfields and the McCoys*. Chapel Hill: University of North Carolina Press.

Jones, S. (1975). "The Lessons of Wage and Price Controls." In *Wage and Price Controls*, J. Kraft and B. Roberts, eds. New York: Praeger Publishers.

Katsenelinboigen, A. (1977). "Coloured Markets in the Soviet Union." *Soviet Studies* 29(1): 62–85.

Katz, A., and E. Bender. (1976). *The Strength in Us: Self-help Groups in the Modern World*, New York: Franklin Watt.

Katzner, D. W. (1983). *Analysis Without Measurement*. New York: Cambridge University Press.

Kirzner, I. M. (1973). *Competition and Entrepreneurship*. Chicago: The University of Chicago Press.

Kirzner, I. M. (1981). "The 'Austrian' Perspective." In *The Crisis in Economic Theory*, D. Bell and I. Kristol, eds. New York: Basic Books.

Klockars, C. (1974). *The Professional Fence*. New York: The Free Press.

Knight, B. and R. Hayes. (1982). *The Self-help Economy: Social and Economic Development in the Inner City*. London: Voluntary Services Council.

Knight, F. H. (1921). *Risks, Uncertainty and Profit*. Houghton Mifflin.

Kunreuther, H. (1978). *Disaster Insurance Protection: Public Policy Lessons*. New York: John Wiley and Sons, Inc.

Lasch, C. (1977). *Haven in a Heartless World: The Family Besieged*. New York: Basic Books.

Lee, R. (1968). "What Hunters Do for a Living, or, How to Make Out on Scarce Resources." In *Man the Hunter*, R. Lee and I. Devore, eds. Chicago: Aldine.

Lee, R. (1969). "!Kung Bushman Subsistence: An Input-Output Analysis." In *Environment and Cultural Behavior*, A. Vayda, ed. Garden City, N.Y.: Natural History Press.

Leibenstein, H. (1976). *Beyond Economic Man*. Cambridge, Mass.: Harvard University Press.

Leijonhuhvud, A. (1973). "Effective Demand Failures." *Swedish Journal of Economics* 75(1): 27–58.

Lerner, A. (1944). *The Economics of Control*. New York: Macmillan.

Lewis, O. (1951). *Life in a Mexican Village: Tepoztlan Revisited*. Urbana: University of Illinois Press.

Libman-Rubenstein, R. E. (1979). "Group Violence in America: Its Structure and Limitations." In *Violence in America*, H. D. Graham and T. R. Gurr, eds. Beverly Hills: Sage Publications.

Liebow, E. (1967). *Talley's Corner: A Study of Negro Corner Men*. Boston: Little, Brown.

Lieven, A. (December 14, 1989). "Economist Seen as Prague's Most Trusted Leader." *The Times* 8.

Lomnitz, L. (1971). "Reciprocity of Favors in the Urban Middle Class of Chile." *Studies in Economic Anthropology* 10: 93–106.

Łoś, M., ed. (1990). *The Second Economy in Marxist States*. London: Macmillan Press.

Lowenthal, M. (1975). "The Social Economy in Urban Working Class Communities." In *The Social Economy of Cities*, G. Gappert and H. Ross, eds., pp. 447–69. Beverly Hills: Sage Publications.

Lowenthal, M. (1981). "Non-Market Transactions in an Urban Community." In *Informal Institutions*, S. Henry, ed. New York: St. Martin's Press.

Macaulay, S. (1963). "Non-Contractual Relations in Business: A Preliminary Study." *American Sociological Review* 28: 55–66.

Maine, H. S. (1861). *Ancient Law*. London: J. Murray.

Malinowski, B. (1922). *Argonauts of the Western Pacific*. London: Routledge.

Margolis, S. E. (April, 1985). "The Excess Capacity Controversy: A Critique of Recent Criticism." *Economic Inquiry* 24:265–75.

Mars, G. (1982). *Cheats at Work: An Anthropology of Workplace Crime*. London: George Allen and Unwin.

Mars, G., and Y. Altman. (1983a). "The Cultural Bases of Soviet Georgia's Second Economy." *Soviet Studies* 35(4): 546–60.

Mars, G., and Y. Altman. (1983b). "How a Soviet Economy Really Works: Cases and Implications." In *Corruption: Causes, Consequences, and Control*, Michael Clarke, ed. London: Frances Pinter.

Mars, G., and M. Nicod. (1984). *The World of Waiters*. London: George Allen and Unwin.

Marshall, A. (1961). *Principles of Economics*, 8th ed. London: Macmillan.

Marx, K. (1842). "Proceedings of the Sixth Rhine Province Assembly. Third Article. Debates on the Law of the Theft of Wood." Reprinted in K. Marx and F. Engels, (1975). *Collected Works Vol.1*. New York: International Publishers.

Mauss, M. (1925). *Essai Sur Le Don. (The Gift)*. Translated by Ian Cunnison. London: Cohen and West.

McCloskey, D. N. (December, 1986). "The Open Fields of England: Rent, Risk, and the Role of Interest, 1300–1815." Paper presented at the American Economic Association—Econometric Society Meetings, New Orleans.

Meeks-Lowery, S. (Winter, 1987). "LETS—A Community Barter System at Work." *Building Economic Alternatives: Self-Reliant Community Development* 14.

Milward, A. S. (1984). *The Reconstruction of Western Europe: 1945–1951*, London: Methuen & Co., Ltd.

Mingione, E. (1985). "Social Reproduction of the Surplus Labour Force: The Case of 'Southern Italy.' " In *Beyond Employment*, N. Redclift and E. Mingione, eds. Oxford: Blackwell.

Mintz, S. (1961). "Pratik." In *Patterns of Land Utilization and Other Papers*, V. E. Garfield, ed. Seattle: University of Washington Press.

Montandon, G. (1934). "Traité d'ethnologie Culturelle." Cited in A. H. Quiggin. *A Survey of Primitive Money*. (1949) London: Methuen.

Montgomery, W. D. (1972). "Markets in Licenses and Efficient Pollution Control Programs." *Journal of Economic Theory* 5 (4):395–418.

Moser, C. (1978). "Informal Sector or Petty Commodity Production: Dualism or Dependence in Urban Development?" *World Development* 6: 1042–64.

Nash, M. (1961). "The Social Context of Economic Choice in a Small Society." *Man* (N.S.) 61 (219): 186–91.

Nash, M. (1964). "The Organization of Economic Life." In *Horizons of Anthropology*, S. Tax, ed. Austin: University of Texas Press.

Nash, R. (1967). *Wilderness and the American Mind*. New Haven, Conn.: Yale University Press.

Nelson, J. (1992). "Gender, Metaphor, and the Definition of Economics." *Economics and Philosophy* 8(1): forthcoming.

Niskanen, W. (1979). *Bureaucracy and Representative Government*. Chicago: Aldine-Atherton.

Olmstead, A. L., and P. Rhode. (1985). "Rationing Without Government: The West Coast Gas Famine of 1920." *American Economic Review* 15(5): 1044–1082.

Olson, M. (1963). *The Economics of Wartime Shortage*. Durham, N.C.: Duke University Press.

Olson, M. (1965). *The Logic of Collective Action*. Cambridge, Mass.: Harvard University Press.

Pahl, R. E. (1984). *Divisions of Labour*. Oxford: Basil Blackwell.

Pahl, R. E., and C. Wallace. (1985). "Household Work Strategies in Economic Recession." In *Beyond Employment: Household, Gender, and Subsistence*, N. Redclift and E. Mingione, eds. Oxford: Basil Blackwell.

Parsons, T., and N.J. Smelser. (1956). *Economy and Society: A Study in the Integration of Economic and Social Theory*. Glencoe, Ill.: Free Press.

Peltzman, S. (1976). "Toward a More General Theory of Regulation." *Journal of Law and Economics* 19(2): 211–40.

Plott, C. R. (1986). "Laboratory Experiments in Economics: The Implications of Posted-Price Institutions." *Science* 232: 732–38.

Pohlman, J. E. (1975). "Price Controls: Lessons from Recent Experience." In *Wage and Price Controls*, J. Kraft and B. Roberts, eds. New York: Praeger Publishers.

Polanyi, K. (1957). *The Great Transformation*. Boston: Beacon Press.

Portes, A., and J. Borocz. (1988). "The Informal Sector Under Capitalism and State Socialism: A Preliminary Comparison." *Social Justice* 15: 17–28.

Portes, A., M. Castells, and L. A. Benton, eds. (1989). *The Informal Economy: Studies in Advanced and Less Developed Countries*. Baltimore, Md.: Johns Hopkins University Press.

Pospisil, L. (1963). *Kapauku Papuan Economy*. New Haven, Conn.: Yale University Publications in Anthropology 67.

Quiggin, A. H. (1949). *A Survey of Primitive Money*. London: Methuen.

Radford, R. A. (1945). "The Economic Organization of a P.O.W. Camp." *Economica* 12. Reprinted in *Readings in Economics*, P.A. Samuelson, ed., 6th ed. New York: McGraw Hill.

Rappaport, R. A. (1968). *Pigs for the Ancestors: Ritual of the Ecology of a New Guinea People*. New Haven, Conn.: Yale University Press.

Rayner, S. (1988). "The Rules that Keep Us Equal." In *Rules, Decisions, and Inequality in Egalitarian Societies*, J. G. Flanagan and S. Rayner, eds. Aldershot, U.K.: Gower.

Rayner, S., and R. Cantor. (1987). "How Fair is Safe Enough? The Cultural Approach to Societal Technology Choice." *Risk Analysis* 7: 3–9.

Redclift, M. (1987). *Sustainable Development: Exploring the Contradictions*. New York: Methuen.

Redclift, M. (1988). "Sustainable Development and the Market: A Framework for Analysis." *Futures* 20(6): 635–50.

Renner, C. (1949). *The Institutions of Private Law and Their Social Functions*. London: Routledge and Kegan Paul.

Roberts, B., R. Finnegan, and D. Gallie, eds. (1985). *New Approaches to Economic Life*. Manchester, U.K.: Manchester University Press.

Roberts, S. (1979). *Order and Dispute: An Introduction to Anthropology*. Harmondsworth, U.K.: Penguin.

Robinson, D., and S. Henry. (1977) *Self-help and Health: Mutual Aid for Modern Problems*. Oxford: Martin Robertson.

Sah, R. K. (1987). "Queues, Rations, and Markets." *American Economic Review* 77(1): 69–77.

Sahlins, M. (1972). *Stone Age Economics*. Chicago: Aldine-Atherton.

Sampson, S. (1987). "The Second Economy in the Soviet Union and Eastern Europe." *Annals of the American Academy of Political and Social Science* 49(3): 120–36.

Sampson, S. (1988). "'May You Live Only by Your Salary!': The Unplanned Economy in Eastern Europe." *Social Justice* 15(3–4): 135–59.

Schelling, T. C. (1978). *Micromotives and Macrobehavior*. New York: W. W. Norton.

Scherer, F. M. (1970). *Industrial Market Structure and Economic Performance*. Chicago: Rand McNally.

Scherer, F. M. (1980). *Industrial Market Structure and Economic Performance*, 2d ed. Chicago: Rand-McNally.

Schneider, H. K. (1974). *Economic Man: The Anthropology of Economics*. New York: The Free Press.

Schotter, A. (1985). *Free Market Economics*. New York: St. Martin's Press.

Schumpeter, J. A. (1942). *Capitalism, Socialism, and Democracy*. New York: Harper & Row.

Schumpeter, J. A. (1964). *Business Cycles*. New York: McGraw-Hill.

Scott, J. C. (1976). *The Moral Economy of the Peasant*, New Haven, Conn.: Yale University Press.

Settle, W. A. (1966). *Jesse James Was His Name: Or Fact and Fiction Concerning the Careers of the Notorious James Brothers of Missouri*. Columbia: University of Missouri Press.

Shearing, C., and P. Stenning, eds. (1987). *Private Policing*. Beverly Hills: Sage Publications.

Shepherd, W. G. (1979). *The Economics of Industrial Organization*. Englewood Cliffs, N.J.: Prentice-Hall, Inc.

Siegel, B. J. (1979). "Defensive Cultural Adaptation." In *Violence in America*, M. D. Graham and T. R. Gurr, eds., pp. 455–72. Beverly Hills: Sage Publications.

Simmel, G. (1907). *The Philosophy of Money*. Translated by T. Bottomore and D. Frisby, 1978. Boston: Routledge and Kegan Paul.

Simon, H. (February, 1955). "A Behavioral Model of Rational Choice." *Quarterly Journal of Economics* 69: 99–118.

Simon, H. (1961). *Administrative Behavior*, 2d ed. New York: Macmillan. (Originally published in 1947.)

Simonis, U. E. (1990). *Beyond Growth: Elements of Sustainable Development*. Berlin: Edition Sigma Bohn.

Singh Uberoi, J. P. (1962). *Politics of the Kula Ring*. Manchester, U.K.: Manchester University Press.

Smith, A. (1776). *The Wealth of Nations*. London: W. Strahan. Reprinted in 1922. London: J. M. Dent & Sons.

Smith, J. D. (1987). "Measuring the Informal Economy." In *The Annals: The Informal Economy*, L. A. Ferman, S. Henry, and M. Hoyman, eds., pp. 83–99. Beverly Hills: Sage Publications.

Smith, J. K., and R. L. Smith. (January, 1985). "A Theory of Ex Post Versus Ex Ante Price Determination." *Economic Inquiry* 23: 57–67.

Smith, V. (May, 1974). "Economic Theory and Its Discontents." *American Economic Review* 64: 320–22.

Smith, V. (1986). "Experimental Methods in the Political Economy of Exchange." *Science* 234: 167–73.

Sonnichsen, C. L. (1986). *Roy Bean: Law West of the Pecos.* Albuquerque: University of New Mexico Press.

South, N. (1988). *Policing for Profit: The Private Security Sector and the New Division of Policing Labour.* Beverly Hills: Sage Publications.

Stack, C. B. (1974). *All Our Kin: Strategies for Survival in a Black Community.* New York: Harper & Row.

Stevenson, G. (1984). *The Swiss Grazing Commons: A Case Study in Common Property Resource Economics,* Ph.D. diss. Madison: University of Wisconsin.

Stigler, G. J. (1971). "The Theory of Economic Regulation." *Bell Journal of Economics and Management Science* 2: 3–21.

Stiglitz, J. E. (April, 1974). "Incentives and Risk Sharing in Sharecropping." *Review of Economic Studies* 41: 219–55.

Stiglitz, J. E., (1983). "Risk, Incentives and Insurance: The Pure Theory of Moral Hazard." *The Geneva Papers on Risk and Insurance* 8(26): 4–33.

Stiglitz, J. E. (1986). "Theory of Competition, Incentives, and Risk." In *New Developments in the Analysis of Market Structure,* J. E. Stiglitz and G. F. Mathewson, eds. Cambridge, Mass: MIT Press.

Stone, A. (1982). *Regulation and Its Alternatives.* Washington, D.C.: Congressional Quarterly Press.

Strathern, A. (1971). *The Rope of Moka: Big-men and Ceremonial Exchange in Mount Hagen.* New York: Cambridge University Press.

Styles, J. (1983). "Embezzlement, Industry, and the Law in England, 1500–1800." In *Manufacture in Town and Country Before the Factory,* M. Berg et al., eds. New York: Cambridge University Press.

Swedberg, R. (1987). "Economic Sociology." *Current Sociology* 35 (1–221).

The Times. (December 30, 1989). "Polish M.P.'s Accept Harsh Package for Economic Revolution," 11.

Tollison, R. D. (1982). "Rent-Seeking: A Survey." *KYKLOS* 35:575–602.

Tonnies, F. (1887). *Gemeinschaft und Geselleschaft.* (*Community and Society*). Translated by L. Fues, 1957. East Lansing: Michigan State University Press.

Toumanoff, P. G. (1984). "A Positive Analysis of the Theory of Market Failure." *KYKLOS* 37: 529–41.

Trevisian, D. (December 18, 1989). "Yugoslav Party Ready to Quit if Reforms Blocked." *The Times,* 7.

Umbeck, J. (1976). *A Theoretical and Empirical Investigation into the Formation of Property Rights: The California Gold Rush.* Ph.D. diss. University of Washington.

Umbeck, J. (1981). "Might Makes Right: A Theory of the Formation and Initial Distribution of Property Rights." *Economic Inquiry* 19(1): 38–59.

U.S. Department of Energy. (October, 1989). *Report to the Congress of the United States—A Compendium of Options for Government Policy to Encourage Private Sector Responses to Potential Climate Changes.* Vol. 1: Methodological Justification and Generic Policy Instruments.

Varian, H. R., (1978). *Microeconomic Analysis.* New York: W. W. Norton.

Wallerstein, I. (1974). *The Modern World System: Capitalist Agriculture and the*

Origins of the European World Economy in the Sixteenth Century. London: Academic Press.

Wallerstein, I. (1979). *The Capitalist World Economy*. Cambridge, Mass.: Cambridge University Press.

Ward, C. (1981). "Community Education." In *Informal Institutions*, S. Henry, ed. New York: St. Martin's Press.

Weiss, L. (1987). "Explaining the Underground Economy: State and Social Structure." *The British Journal of Sociology* 38: 216–34.

Whyte, W. F. (1955). *Street Corner Society*. Chicago: University of Chicago Press.

Williamson, O. E. (1975). *Markets and Hierarchies: Analysis and Antitrust Implications*. New York: Free Press.

Williamson, O. E. (1979). "Transaction-Cost Economics: The Governance of Contractual Relations." *Journal of Law and Economics* 22: 3–61.

Williamson, O. E. (1985). *The Economic Institutions of Capitalism*. New York: Free Press.

Wilson, J. A. (1980). "Adaptation to Uncertainty and Small Members Exchange: The New England Fresh Fish Market." *The Bell Journal of Economics* 7(2): 491–504.

Winter, Jr., S. G. (1963). "Economic Viability after Thermonuclear War: The Limits of Feasible Production." *Rand Memorandum*, RM–3436–PR. Santa Monica, Calif.: The Rand Corp.

Winter, Jr., S. G. (1968). "The Federal Role in Postattack Economic Organization." In *Proceedings of the Symposium on Postattack Recovery from Nuclear War*. Washington, D. C.: National Academy of Sciences.

Zeitlin, L. R. (1971). "Stimulus Response: A Little Larceny Can Do a Lot for Employee Morale." *Psychology Today* 5: 22, 24, 64.

Index

About the Authors

ROBIN CANTOR, an economist, is program director of Decision, Risk, and Management Science at the National Science Foundation.

STUART HENRY is associate professor of sociology at Eastern Michigan University. He is the author of several books, including *Informal Institutions: Alternative Networks in the Corporate State* (1981), *Private Justice: Toward Integrated Theorizing in the Sociology of Law* (1983), and *The Informal Economy* (1987).

STEVE RAYNER is senior program manager at Oak Ridge National Laboratory. He is the author of several books, including *Rules, Decisions, and Inequality in Egalitarian Societies* (1988) and *Energy Policies and the Greenhouse Effect* (1991).